* youth: self-concept and behavior

97

james c. hansen
state university of new york
at buffalo

peter e. maynard
university of rhode island

charles e. merrill publishing company
a bell & howell company
columbus, ohio

* counseling youth series

under the editorship of

herman peters

the ohio state university

Published by
Charles E. Merrill
Publishing Company
A Bell & Howell Company
Columbus, Ohio 43216

International Standard Book Number: 0-675-09048-2

Library of Congress Catalog Card Number: 72-89666

1 2 3 4 5 6 7 8 — 78 77 76 75 74 73

Printed in the United States of America

preface

This book is about the self-concept and behavior of youth. A person's self-concept is an important influence on his behavior and his behavior and other's reactions to it are important influences on his self-concept. A cycle effect is apparent. An individual generally behaves in ways consistent with his self-concept. In striving to be consistent with his self-concept he emits behavior for which he is rewarded or punished, thus enhancing, damaging or reinforcing his prevailing self-concept. This cycle is generally repetitive unless one of the factors is somehow changed. This book examines the process of self-concept development, the interrelationship of self-concept and behavior, and ways of enhancing one's self-concept and changing behavior patterns.

There are various conceptulations of the self-concept which are presented in Chapter One. We propose a view of self-concept gleaned from a social psychological perspective. A child learns his self-concept from others. A self-concept is formed from early social interactions with significant individuals and later influenced by continued feedback from others. The individual reacts to his internal interpretation of the social interactions and behaves according to his perceptions. Behavior and self-concepts are not simply a product of what has happened to the person from the outside but are also a result of how he feels about himself on the inside. Chapter Two examines the process of self-concept development in youth. The focus is on the influence of other people and the youth's interpretation of situations which can facilitate or deter self-esteem. Some examples of the relationship between self-concept and behavior are presented in Chapter Three. The youth's past experience will have a vast influence on his present self-concept and behavior. Chapter Four focuses on enhancing the youth's perception of himself and helping to change his present behavior. Additional attention is given to changing the environment in ways that can help a youth to learn who he is and to develop self-esteem and effective behavior.

We certainly acknowledge the concepts and research of the many people who have influenced our ideas in presenting this material. We appreciate the stimulating thinking of our students and colleagues. A special thanks goes to Esther Kirdani for her research and editorial assistance.

J.C.H.
P.E.M.

contents

one   *   concepts of self-concept   1

two   *   development of self-concept   26

three   *   self-concept and behavior   53

four   *   the counselor and self-concept   77

name index   102

subject index   105

one * concepts of self-concept

It would seem that from time immemorial man has been asking and pondering over the questions, "Who am I?" and "What am I?" Very early in his history man began to think of what we today call the self. It took on various labels, but the conception of an inner driving force which influences one's behavior seems to pervade first the folk literature and later the more formal and chronologized writings across many cultures.

early concepts of self

Psychology as a formal field of study is still quite youthful. Therefore, to trace some of the earliest formal writings on the concept of self, contributions from other fields of study must be examined. The religious writings of early man reflect the belief that man has some inner regulatory agent which influences his destiny. These writings speak of a *soul* or an inner being which has spiritual qualities and thus is a separate entity from the material body (Donceel, 1955). However, the philosophical writings of ancient times speak more to the point of the *self*, as it has come to be known. The Grecian philosophies provide one of the first records of a concept similar to that of the self. Plato, in the *Phaedo*, described the soul as the initiator of activity—conscious, lifegiving, and non-material.

1

He really was talking more of a self than a soul as we understand these terms. Following Plato, Aristotle in the third century B.C. conducted a systematic and logical enquiry into the nature of the ego.

Augustine (354-430 A.D.) and Thomas Aquinas (1100 A.D.), who were combination philosophers and theologians, delved deeply into the essence of the inner self. Theologically, they were two of the foremost Christians writing on the nature of God and of man. Interestingly, their philosophical leanings were quite different. Augustine followed mostly Platonic thinking, while Aquinas was basically Aristotelian. Viney (1969) notes that Augustine, in his *Confessions*, provided the first glimpse of introspection into the personal self. Aquinas' epistemological writings (Van Stienberghen, 1949) provided us with extensive exposition on the question of self-knowledge.

In 1644, René Descartes published his *Principles of Philosophy*, which provided a significant turning point in man's thinking about his non-material nature. In the intervening years between Aquinas and Descartes the question of self-knowledge remained a rhetorical one, since most of the philosophical writing was bogged down in religious dogma. A rapidly changing Europe of the seventeenth century provided a background and a readiness for Descartes' *cogito ergo sum* (I think, therefore I exist) and his principle of universal doubt. In introducing doubt as a principal tool of disciplinary inquiry, Descartes concluded he could not doubt that he doubted. If he was doubting, he must be thinking, and if he was thinking, he must exist.

Several other philosophers of this period also expounded upon the centrality of the inner "self" in systems of cognition and consciousness. On the continent, Spinoza and Leibnitz added their ideas about the mystery of the non-physical aspects of man (Purkey, 1970). Meanwhile, the English philosophers, Hobbes, Locke, and Hume, all were probing the nature of the self. Hobbes advanced a code of ethics based on self-interest; Locke conceived man as "a thinking intelligent being, that has reason and reflection, and can consider self as itself." Hume concentrated on an examination of personal identity (Viney, 1960). In summarizing the writing on the self in the seventeenth and eighteenth centuries, Purkey (1970) notes, "terms such as mind, soul, psyche and self were often used interchangeably, with scant regard for an invariant vocabulary or scientific experimentation. For the most part, a general state of confusion in regard to the concept of self existed into this present century."

early conceptions of self in psychology

Psychology as a recognizable and separate discipline didn't emerge until the end of the nineteenth century. The two major impetuses for this were the writings of Sigmund Freud and William James. Interestingly, these two also were very prominent in formulating conceptions about the self and the ego, and their early conceptualizations laid the groundwork for several of the later self theories that emerged. James, in his two-volume work *The Principles of Psychology* (1890), devoted an entire chapter to "the consciousness of self," which was the longest of any in his two volumes. It would be proper to say that much of the contemporary theorizing about self-concept derives from William James. He considered ego the individual's sense of identity. In addition to this global concept, James saw the self as including spiritual, material, and social aspects.

Freud's writings were a significant breakthrough in man's quest to understand internal processes. Freud gave much attention to self-understanding, under the rubric of ego development and functioning. Monroe (1955) has suggested that the Freudians and neo-Freudians generally hesitate to elevate the self to the status of a primary psychological unit or give it a central position in their theoretical formulations.

In the late 1920's, the lines of demarcation among schools of psychological thought, especially in America, were being clearly drawn. Advocates of one or another of the organized schools felt compelled to disagree with the opposing ones. For instance, the Freudians emphasized unconscious motivation; the introspectionists rallied around the process of introspection as *the* way to explore consciousness; the gestaltists exalted the value of insight and emphasized the selective perceiver; and the behaviorists were busy discrediting the other systems of psychological thought and turned their attention almost exclusively to the study of observable behavior, claiming only this was fit for scientific inquiry. Appealing to the scientific method of studying phenomena, they advocated and espoused the strict hypothesis testing model of the natural sciences.

Thus J. B. Watson and his partners in the behavioral school, in the tradition of good behaviorists, manipulated the bulk of psychologists in America away from the abstract and hard-to-measure concepts such as self, ego strength, awareness, and other processes dealing with the inner life of the individual, to observable stimuli and responses. Fuzzy inner-directed perceptions were seen as being outside the realm of scientific psychology.

Wylie (1961) notes that during the second, third, and fourth decades of the twentieth century, constructs concerning the self did not receive much acclaim or attention from the behavioral and functional schools of psychology, which at that point in time were definitely holding center stage. As Hilgard (1949) points out, the introspectionists could not handle the self, and "mentalistic" constructs such as self-concept were blasphemous to the behaviorists.

Concurrently, the Freudians and neo-Freudians had developed some psychodynamic postulates which necessarily implied a self-referent to make them plausible and understandable. However, for at least two reasons, these theorists retarded the bringing of constructs concerned with the self to the fore. First of all, Freud himself, in his early theorizing, concentrated on the role of the id, and he never explicitly formulated a self-concept, nor did he assign a high value to the closely related ego functions. Second, his theory was under heavy attack in America by many general psychologists who found it lacking in vigor and not too susceptible to empirical testing.

An interesting phenomenon that accompanied each swing from self-theory to behavioral theory is that education also made the switch each time. In this century in America the impact of psychologists upon education and teaching is clearly evident. As the pendulum swung from Freud's and James' stress on the ego and self-functions to Watson's stance on observable and measurable behaviors, so too the schools of education swung. Even to this day it is occurring. During the decade from 1955 to 1965, there was much writing and research in psychology on self-perceptions, self-concepts, and other such constructs. Starting about 1965 and carrying into today, the pendulum has swung again to the behavioral side. Note that such concepts as accountability and performance contracting are capturing a prominent place in the professional journals and at professional meetings of educators.

Throughout the twenties and thirties and into the forties, Watson and the other behaviorists remained both vocal and visual, and represented the predominant view in American psychology. As Wylie (1961) points out, from the 1920's through the 1940's the self received scant attention from the behavioral-oriented psychologists who dominated American psychology. This, despite the fact that George Herbert Mead's *Mind, Self and Society* appeared in 1934. Even though Mead's writings on the self were to become influencial and well-thought-of, the behaviorists, with their strong emphasis on observable stimuli and response, managed to downplay such internal constructs as self, mind, and consciousness.

Other psychologists (Lewin, 1935; Goldstein, 1937) were discussing the self in the 1930's. However, it was not until the following decade that the concept of self again became an important rallying point. There are a number of influences that can account for this resurgence of interest. Freud, in his later writings, began to assign greater importance to ego development and functioning, and the neo-Freudians emphasized the importance of the self picture and the self ideal. Concurrently, American psychologists were entering the arena of the clinic. They found the behavioral models too restrictive to account for the phenomena they were observing. Since their interests were somewhat different from those of the general experimental psychologists of cognition and motivation, the clinicians saw less need for neat and sophisticated theorizing. Rather, they were searching for conceptual models which accounted for their observations.

Foremost among the clinical psychologists who were objecting to behaviorism as too narrow and too passive to account for most human behavior was Carl Rogers. He acquired a substantial following and built a dynasty that, to be sure, Rogers himself never envisioned. Rogers' theory was so involved with the client's feeling about his self-worth and self-dignity that it has come to be called "self-theory."

Another very significant contribution and influence in the reintroduction of the self into psychology and education was the writing of Combs and Snygg. In their 1949 book, *Individual Behavior*, they stressed the importance of the maintenance and enhancement of the self. Furthermore, they concluded that all behavior is dependent upon the individual's personal frame of reference. ". . . behavior is determined by the totality of experience of which an individual is aware at an instant of action, his 'phenomenal field.'"

Wylie (1961) noted the significant increase in the interest and research on several inner-directed constructs, but especially on self-concept. In her *Self-Concept: A Critical Survey of the Pertinent Research Literature*, Wylie defined her domain as being "broadly conceived to include studies of pertinence to a wide variety of theories which accord an important or even a central role to self-concept." Under this rubric, she placed Adler, 1924; Angyal, 1941; Freud, 1950; Fromm, 1939; Horney, 1937; Lecky, 1945; Lynd, 1958; Maslow, 1954; Mean, 1934; McClellan, 1951;

Rogers, 1951a; Snygg and Combs, 1949; Sullivan, 1947. Lecky (1945), Snygg and Combs (1949), and Rogers (1951) have been labeled phenomenologists because of their stress on the role of the conscious self-concept in determining a person's behavior.

Since the late 1950's, the interest in self-theory and the dynamic of the self continued to be prominent in the literature (Brookover, 1962, 1964, 1965; Combs, 1965; Diggory, 1966; Coopersmith, 1967). In the area of vocational psychology, which neither Wylie (1961) nor several other authors who have summarized the research and writing on self-concept included, there has been a substantial amount of research on the vocational manifestation of self. The work of Donald Super and his collaborators and, to a lesser extent, Tiedeman and O'Hara has been addressed to the development of vocational self-concept. In 1963, Super, Stavishevsky, Matlin, and Jordaan clarified and expanded the theory that vocational choice is the implementation of one's self-concept.

Thus the interest in self-theory and self-concept is very prominent even today. Several authors have recently produced books which relate self-concept theory to the educational enterprise. La Benne and Greene (1969) explore the merits and consequences of teaching activities in terms of their probable influence on a child's developing self-concept. Purkey (1970) examines the strong and persistent relationship between self and academic achievement and shows why there is a deepening discontent with the notion that human ability is the overwhelming factor in academic achievement. Hamachek (1971), in a more extensive work, looks at self-understanding, self-consistency, how self-concept is linked to physical growth and development, how it is connected to academic adjustment, and how the healthy self-image develops.

specific theorists and the self

There are several different ways to divide the theorists who have been concerned with the self or its various facets. We have chosen to utilize three categories: the pioneers, the phenomenologists, and the social psychologists. Admittedly, these are not perfectly clear-cut distinctions. For instance, not to place Cooley, who wrote about the *Looking Glass Self* in 1902, in the pioneer category seems strange. Likewise, to place Gordon Allport in the pioneer category rather than with the social psychologists also seems strange. The reasons for these placements are that Cooley, even though writing quite early, had a limited impact on those writing and researching on the self, except for those in social psychology. On the other hand, Allport differs in several ways from the social psychologists and generally has had an impact on others in psychology and education who have been working on self-concept.

the pioneers

william james. It would be appropriate to conclude that a significant amount of the past and current theorizing about self-concept is derived from or related to the world of William James. His definition of self was ". . . in its widest possible sense . . . a man's self is the sum total of all he can call his" (James, 1890, p. 291). For James, the empirical self, or *me*, is made up of three distinct constituents: the *material self*, or body, clothes and possessions; the *social self* or the opinions and knowledge a person's peers have of him; and the *spiritual self*, or inner being of abilities and traits. These are presided over by the ego, which is the unifying entity in one's personality. It is the person's ego that gives him his identity by its executive function and power to pull all the selves together into a meaningful arrangement.

James clearly meant the self to have dynamic qualities. In fact, James gave the self a dynamic quality in terms of self-preservation and seeking. "From James, then, came a view of self which incorporated feelings and attitudes along with a principle of causality" (La Benne and Greene, 1969).

The topic of personal identity which James closely related to his self received ample attention in *The Principles of Psychology* (1890). The contribution of James to this notion reflected his formulations of the stream of consciousness and attention. "The sense of our own personal identity, then, is exactly like any one of our perceptions of sameness among phenomena. It is a conclusion grounded either on the resemblance in a fundamental respect, or on the continuity before the mind, of the phenomena compared" (p. 334).

sigmund freud. Unlike James, Freud was not formally concerned with self-image and self-identity. Rather, for Freud, many of the duties and functions other theorists catalogue under the self-concept are the function and duties of the ego. Freud saw personality as made up of three major systems, the *id, ego,* and *superego.* Any human behavior is nearly always the product of an interaction among these three systems; rarely does one system operate to the exclusion of the other two.

However, the ego is the executive of the personality because it controls the gateways to action, selects the features of the environment to which it will respond, and decides what instincts will be satisfied and in what manner.

The ego maintains a psychic balance between the demands of the person's moral inclinations (the superego) and the natural impulses (the id). The ego has to check both the id and the superego if it is to govern the personality wisely, yet it must have enough energy left over to engage in necessary intercourse with the external world.

gordon allport. Throughout his career, Allport intensely studied the complexity and uniqueness of individual human beings. Yet he saw that, while he must do justice to the complexity and uniqueness of each individual person, at the same time he must acknowledge that there was an underlying congruence or unity in man's nature. This led Allport to emphasize those phenomena represented under the terms of *ego* and *self*. Allport calls the ego, or self, functions the appropriate functions of the personality. The proprium comprises awareness of self and striving activities which include bodily sense, self-image, self-esteem, and identity, as well as thinking and knowing (La Benne and Greene, 1969).

the phenomenologists

The second group of theorists we will discuss are the phenomenologists. For the phenomenologist, reality is not in the event, but in the phenomenon; that is, the person's perception of the event. One's perceptions grow out of one's experiences. The phenomenological theorists to be discussed are Snygg and Combs, Rogers, and Maslow. These theorists concentrate very heavily on the subjective side of the self. While they recognize there is a self-as-object, they de-emphasize it. The self, then, as they define it, is heavily weighted on the side of self-as-subject.

snygg and combs. Combs and Snygg (1959) believe that the individual is a living, active organism engaged in organizing its world. The organization which the individual gives to the world is known as his perceptual or phenomenal field. This is more than the area of sensory perception, including cognition, conceptions, and knowledge. The phenomenological field is the universe, including the individual himself, as it is perceived and experienced by him. An individual can only know the world through his perception and there is no reality for the individual other than what constitutes his perceptions or phenomenological field. "What is perceived is not what exists, but what one believes exists" (p. 84). The individual acts only on the basis of his perceptions, his phenomenal field. Combs and Snygg state that "all behavior, without exception, is completely determined by, and pertinent to, the perceptual field of the behaving organism." (p. 20). The self is a part of the individual's phenomenal field. It includes all of the perceptions, conceptions, attitudes, and beliefs he has about himself. The phenomenal self is the real self in terms of the person's behavior. The phenomenal self is the most important part of the phenomenal field since it is the pivotal part of the field around which perceptions are organized. "All perceptions . . . derive their meaning from their relation to the phenomenal self" (p. 131). "What a person thinks and how he behaves are largely determined by the concepts he holds about himself and his abilities" (p. 122). The centrality of the self in phenomenology is indicated by the postulate that a single motive for behavior is the preservation and enhancement of the phenomenal self.

carl rogers. Rogers' theory of personality represents a synthesis of phenomenology as represented by Snygg and Combs, of holistic and organismic theory as developed in the writings of Goldstein, Maslow, Angyal, and Sullivan's interpersonal theory, combined with a self-theory.

The self is a differentiated portion of the phenomenal field and consists of a pattern of conscious perceptions and values of the "I" and "me." The self, which is at the nucleus of Rogers' theory of personality, has five important and distinct properties: It develops out of the organism's interaction with the environment. It may introject the values of others and perceive them in a distorted fashion. The self strives for consistency. The organism behaves in ways which are consistent with the self, and experiences that are not consistent with the self-structure are perceived as threats.

Following Snygg and Combs, Rogers (1951) states, "a portion of the total perceptual field gradually becomes differentiated as the self" (p. 497). He asserts that a phenomenal self is differentiated out of the entire phenomenal field. The self is the awareness of one's being and functioning. In other words, it is at the same time both the self-as-object, the "me," and the self-as-process, the "I."

How does the individual begin to learn about his self? This occurs when the person begins to interact with the environment and to distinguish what is his and what is the environment's. As soon as the infant begins to interact with his environment, he begins to become aware of himself as an entity separate from the events around him. As the child grows older he begins to notice and think about attributes of himself and the things he does. Events become symbolized in awareness as images and words. Rogers (1959) calls awareness of such events self-experience (p. 223). These awarenesses are the raw material out of which habitual patterns of attending to and thinking about self-characteristics develop. These habitual patterns of thought about the self are for Rogers the self-concept. It includes not only thoughts, such as "I am skinny," but thoughts relating oneself to others, such as "others like me," and thoughts identifying one's relationship with other kinds of events, such as "I am a good tennis partner."

the social psychologists

The third category of theorists who have contributed significantly or concentrated heavily on the development and manifestations of self-concept is further subdivided into two categories for better clarity. The first group we shall discuss under the rubric of social psychologists are practitioner-theorists, namely Alfred Adler, Karen Horney, and Harry Stack Sullivan. The second group, C. H. Cooley, George H. Mead, and Erving Goffman, are sociological theorists who approach the formation and development of a self-concept in a somewhat similar but at the same time quite different orientation. Adler, Horney, and Sullivan all held medical degrees and were more or less traditionally trained in the psychoanalytic framework, Adler and Horney in Europe and Sullivan in the United States. They fall into this category of social psychologists because they deviated from the classical psychoanalytic approach to human behavior and moved clearly to refashion psychoanalytic theory along lines dictated by the orientation developed by the social sciences.

Of these three theorists, Alfred Adler is regarded as the ancestral figure of the "new social psychological look" because as early as 1911 he broke with Freud over the issue of sexuality, and proceeded to develop a theory in which social interest and a striving for superiority became two of his mainstays. Later Karen Horney, reacting to the overwhelming instinctivist orientation of psychoanalysis, pressed for an inclusion of social psychological variables in a personality theory. However, Horney could best be called a revisionist or a neo-Freudian. Adler, although he broke with Freud, still was strongly influenced by him throughout his life and writings.

Sullivan was considerably more independent of psychoanalytic influences. Although he earlier used the Freudian framework, later he deviated heavily from this framework and was profoundly influenced by anthropology and social psychology. Sullivan in his theory of interpersonal relations consolidated the position of a personality theory based on social processes.

The other group to be discussed in this section are the sociological theorists, Cooley, Mead, and Goffman. They approach the definition of self and the formation of a self-concept in a very different way. Cooley and Mead are the antecedents of Goffman, who is one of the leading contemporary proponents of symbolic interactionist theory. The interactionist theory of self-concept attempts to explain the conception that the individual has of himself in terms of his interaction with those about him (Kinch, 1967). In very general terms, the theory states that the individual's conception of himself emerges from social interaction and, in turn, guides or influences the behavior of that individual.

alfred adler. In sharp contrast to Freud's major assumption that man's behavior is motivated by inborn instincts, Adler assumed that man is motivated primarily by social urges. Man is inherently a social being who relates himself to other people, engages in cooperative social activities, places social welfare above selfish interest, and acquires a style of life predominantly social in nature. Adler did not say that a man became socialized merely by being exposed to social processes; social interest is innate although the specific types of relationships with people and social institutions which develop are determined by the nature of the society in which a person lives. This emphasis upon the social determinants of behavior which had been overlooked or minimized by Freud was one of Adler's greatest contributions to psychological theory (Hall and Lindzey, 1957).

Another important theme for Adler is that each person develops a certain unique life style or life plan. Everyone has a style of life but no two people develop the same style. For Adler, the major factors determining how a person will develop a life style or life plan are the specific inferiorities, either fantasized or real, that a person has. An individual sets up a certain "life plan" that is directed in such a way as either to overcome the defect or compensate for it. If a child is physically weak, his style of life will take the form of doing those things which produce physical strength. However, this concept was incomplete for Adler. Explanations, like the one which held that Napolean's aggressive style of life was determined by his slight physical build, were too simple and mechanistic; therefore, Adler moved to the dynamic principle of the creative self.

This concept of the creative self became a focal point of Adler's theory. It also became for him a first cause or prime mover, and all his other concepts were subordinate to it. Like all first causes, the creative self is hard to describe. We can see its effects, but we cannot see it. It is something that intervenes between the stimuli acting on the person and the responses he makes to these stimuli. In essence, the doctrine of the creative self asserts that man makes his own personality. It is constructed out of the raw material of heredity and experience. "The creative self is the yeast that acts upon the facts of the world and transforms these facts into a personality that is subjective, dynamic, unified, personal, and uniquely stylized. The creative self gives meaning to life; it creates the goal as well as the means to the goal. The creative self is the active principle of human life, and it is not unlike the older concept of soul" (Hall and Lindzey, 1957, pp. 124-25).

karen horney. Karen Horney shared with Adler the feeling that Freud had accorded biological and genetic factors an excessive role in determining the formation of one's self-concept. She also shared with Adler the view that man's behavior, rather than being instinctive, was primarily learned, and so was remarkably susceptible to change through a lifetime (Horney, 1945). Horney, by proposing that the vast majority of human behavior was learned, and learned in relation to one's socio-cultural environment, necessitated a study of the relationship between one person's behavior and that of another.

For Horney there were two distinct sets of characteristics that led to the normal development of the self-concept. Every human being is born with certain innate determinants of behavior; and every human being acquires or learns many behaviors or qualities.

Although Horney acknowledged the fact of innate differences

in behavior from subject to subject, and recognized that some behavior was determined by such innate events, she saw such factors as having only limited effect on the formation of the self-concept. She apparently felt that little was known about such constitutional determinants, and by contrast considerably more was known about factors involving learning.

Since she subscribed to the general view that the vast majority of man's behavior is acquired through learning, and that this renders most of his behavior potentially modifiable, Horney devoted her energies toward analyzing learned behaviors as the central forces forming and informing the self. She conceived that situational or environmental events with which a person must respond are the important determinants of how learning occurs. The most important sub-class of such events are the behaviors of other people. Thus Horney emphasized interpersonal relationships. What a person learns is most significantly influenced by the manner in which he is treated by others.

Although Horney did offer some contributions on the development of normal behavior, as a practicing psychiatrist she almost exclusively devoted her attention to an analysis of the development of disordered behavior. Much of Horney's writings are devoted to the development of neurotic self-concepts, for she felt that only by fully understanding the developmental and situational factors involved in the onset of a neurotic self-concept can the practitioner begin to aid the client in reversing these tendencies. In her first theoretical statement, *The Neurotic Personality of Our Times* (1937), she presented the contention that neurotic behavior was brought about by cultural factors, and more specifically by disturbances in human relationships. This led Horney to search for the antecedents of disorder in social situations. Many of these, she claimed, could be found within the interpersonal relationships that occurred within the family during the early formative years. For Horney, biological and physiological determinants receded into the background, and situational determinants were correspondingly emphasized (Ford and Urban, 1963).

Consistent with her emphasis on cultural and social factors was Horney's view that complex behavior was most readily understood in terms of the organized patterns of interpersonal responses which the person developed. Horney (1942) listed ten such interpersonal patterns or neurotic trends which she felt were easily identifiable and also significant. An example of such a pattern of interpersonal behavior or neurotic trend is the *Neurotic Need for*

Perfection and Unassailability. The responses which are typical of such a pattern included:

1. Relentless effort for perfection in general
2. Ruminations and self-recriminations
3. Feelings of superiority over others because of self-evaluation of perfection
4. Fear of finding flaws with the self or making mistakes
5. Fear of criticism (pp. 59-60)

Eventually, Horney decided that all such patterns of behavior could be reduced to three main groupings. A person develops patterns of response consistent with the way he views himself when interacting in social situations. The three patterns, which could be equated to what other theorists label as patterns of self-concepts are: moving toward people, moving against people, and moving away from people.

harry stack sullivan.   Sullivan (1953) made outstanding contributions to self-concept theory through his interpersonal theory of psychiatry. Its major tenet is that personality is "the relatively enduring pattern of recurrent interpersonal situations which characterize a human life" (p. 111). Sullivan emphasized interpersonal relationships in the formation of one's self-concept, and he regarded these as yielding the primary data to be used as the self becomes defined. Behavior disorders were conceived as arising from within the context of interrelationships with people. Correspondingly, the treatment of such disorders requires interpersonal conditions. In simple terms, people make people sick — thus it takes people to make them well.

Since our intent here is not to review the entire personality theory of Sullivan, but rather to pull out those elements of his theory that directly related to formation of the self-concept, let us concentrate on the two complex response interrelationships which encompass most of Sullivan's thinking on the self.

The first of these is personifications. They are groups of related symbolic responses (perceptions, recollections, images, and thoughts) which have been acquired as abstracts from extended experiences with the person "personified." These personifications develop in the course of social interaction. For instance, one's "personification of mother" is a complex response that has been acquired after a series of situations in which one interacts with a mother physically or symbolically. Among the most important personifications an individual develops, starting with infancy and carrying on throughout life, is one's personification of himself. Sullivan referred to a three-way view of self that each person develops over time: the *good me*, the *bad me*, and the *not me*. A person gradually develops his self-concept through self-referent responses build upon a history of experiences with himself. The *good me* is a pattern of habitual responses about the self learned in situations wherein satisfaction was derived. Conversely, the *bad me* is a recurrent pattern of self-referent responses learned in association with anxiety-producing situations. The *not me* self-referent responses are typically very unclear and undifferentiated, since they related to experiences of extreme tension, intense anxiety, horror, and loathing. Contrary to response constellations of the *good me* and the *bad me* which later are committed to language, the *not me* is usually beyond discussion in communicative terms and virtually always continues to operate at a vague, imagistic, and non-verbal level.

The second set of response patterns Sullivan proposed that a person develops as he begins to define himself is what he referred to as a "self-system." The name Sullivan attached to the complex response pattern he called the "self-system" is quite misleading. Actually, Sullivan was referring to a smaller subset of behaviors acquired by an individual in the course of his interpersonal relationships which function to avoid and minimize the occurrence of anxiety, rather than a completely defined set of behaviors equal to the self-concept. Because anxiety-producing situations are inevitable, Sullivan felt a person without such a pattern of responses was "beyond imagination." The pattern is learned primarily in interpersonal situations. The problem is that such avoidance behaviors become so well entrenched and part of one's self-concept that they become very hard even to recognize, let alone change.

charles horton cooley. Cooley, writing in 1902, was one of the forerunners of what was to become a very distinct school of sociologists who have minutely examined the idea of self. He was one of the first to write extensively about the person's social milieu as a significant contributor to how a person views himself. Thus, he developed a theory of the self that was concerned primarily with how the self grows as a consequence of interpersonal interactions. Cooley coined the phrase *the looking-glass self* to describe how a person gains a view of himself. According to Cooley "the kind of feeling one has is determined by the attitude toward this attributed to that other mind. A social self of this sort might be called the reflected or looking-glass self.

> Each to each a looking glass
> Reflects the other that doth pass. (Cooley, 1902)

For Cooley, a self idea had three principal elements: the imagination of our appearance to the other person; the imagination of his judgment of that appearance; and some self-feeling, such as pride. It is clear that Cooley viewed the process of an individual's self-appraisal to be greatly influenced by his perception and interpretation of the reaction of other persons to him.

george herbert mead. The self, according to Mead (1939), emerges through a social process of interaction and communication. The self is not in existence at birth, "but arises in the process of social experience . . . through the individual's relations with the entire process and to individuals within the social construct" (p. 139). To Mead the central psychological problem in self-identity centers around the individual's ability to stand outside himself and experience his own modes of behavior. An individual would need to view himself as a subject or object. Only as the individual can take on the attitudes of others toward him and thus objectify his own behavior in social environments can he fully understand himself and then become a subject to himself. "The self, as that which can be an object to itself, is essentially a social structure, and arises in social experience" (Mead, 1934, p. 140). If he is to engage in this self-awareness process of social interaction, the individual may never become a mass-man or "lonely crowd" type. Rather, he must be a thinking and reflective person. Thinking must precede the forming of any intelligent relationship where the mode of action is based on the individual's total picture of the social process. Thinking is inner conversation to Mead and forms the basis for significant "social intercourse" (pp. 141-2). The role of artist, then, necessitates a creative inner awareness of what arouses him and others. A person first sees whether his words "call out in him the responses he wants to call out in others" (p. 148).

Mead calls the community which responds to and interacts with the self "the generalized other." The self must exist in definite relationships to other selves; the self cannot exist in a vacuum. Mead argues against any psychology which attempts to deal with the self as an isolated, independent force.

One of his most distinguishing trademarks, and the one that is most discussed among social psychologists, is Mead's distinction of the *I* and the *me*. Mead defined the *I* and the *me* in relation to the social community for he continually stressed that whenever we act we are simultaneously aware of ourselves. The *I*, then, is the responsive self; the *I* reacts to the attitude of others, while the *me* is the organized set of attitudes which the *I* accepts as social response. The *I* expresses itself through experience and action as the *me*. The *I* is the individual's initiating, thinking, decision-making self which responds to the *me* of the community through acting. The human personality needs an *I* to respond to a *me* which is social experience. Without *I*'s, we would have no communal *me*'s, only a pack of stampeding animals.

Another important tenet emerging from Mead's theory of the self is that, since interaction between the self and society is always in existence, each one of us behaves in a particular way within specific frameworks; therefore, we are transforming ourselves and our social order. Mead (1934) contends that "the relations between social reconstruction and self or personality reconstruction are reciprocal and internal or organic; social reconstruction by individual members of an organized human society entails self or personality reconstruction in some degree or other by each of these individuals. . ." (p. 309). Central to Mead's contribution as a social psychologist is his view that the self cannot be reconstituted without also altering the community and the social relations of the self to others within the community. Social progress, to Mead, is linked to individual progress, growth, and attainment. For if the individual selves do not "keep pace with . . . social reconstruction" there can be no "progressive social changes" or achievements (p. 310).

erving goffman. Goffman has been included as a self theorist for two reasons. He represents the still-emerging symbolic interactionist theory, an orientation which has influenced most American sociologists specializing in social psychology. The historical development of symbolic interactionism has its roots in the rationalism of John Locke, the foreshadowing of the role-taking process of the Scottish Moralists such as John Hume and Adam Smith, the idealist epistemology of Kant, and other diverse sources (Manis and Meltzer, 1967). It emerged as a distinct perspective in social psychology in the work of John Dewey, John Mark Baldwin, William I. Thomas, Florian Znaniecki, and notably the two theorists we have just previously discussed, Charles Horton Cooley and George Herbert Mead. The symbolic interactionist school includes many notable and influential sociologists including the late Manford H. Kuhn, Herbert G. Blumer, Thomas S. McPartland, Howard S. Becker, Anselm L. Strauss, Alfred R. Lindesmith and Robert K. Merton.

Besides the fact that Goffman falls within the symbolic interactionist camp, we also choose to include him as a theorist because he represents the most radical and eye-catching of the several sub-theories that have emerged within the symbolic interactionist orientation. This sub-theory is the dramaturgical school which was initiated by Kenneth Burke and includes Nelson Foote and Gregory Stone, but has been especially developed by Goffman.

According to Goffman, a person's conception of self is always fluid and in transition. The manner in which an individual views himself changes with each situation in which he finds himself. One's identity in a situation is not absolutely given, but is more or less problematic. For instance, if a man is dressed in formal evening attire, thinking that he has been invited to a formal dinner party, but upon entering the room finds everyone in jeans or other casual clothes, this changes his conception of himself. He had expected to be a formal dinner guest, but now he must question this identity and who he is in relation to this situation. Is he a formal dinner guest? Is he at the wrong residence? Why is he formal and the others casual? The person must momentarily draw back — if not physically, then psychologically — so he can reevaluate the problematic situation which has challenged his self-identity. Commitment to a conception of self is the key which unlocks the resources necessary to avoid immobilization whenever problematic situations occur. Doubt of identity or confusion, while it may not cause complete disorientation, certainly drains action of its meaning, and thus limits mobilization of the organic correlates of emotion, drive, and energy which provide the push of motivated action.

A man's self-concept for Goffman is, then, entirely situational. It evolves around two sets of signs or symbols that occur within social interactions. These two radically different kinds of sign activity are the expression he *gives* and the expression he *gives off*. The first involves verbal symbols or their substitutes, which a man uses solely to convey the information that he and others are known to attach to these symbols. This is communication in the traditional and narrow sense. The second involves a wide range of action that others can treat as symptomatic of the actor (Goffman, 1959). Goffman is primarily interested in the second kind of communication. By understanding this more theatrical and contextual kind of communication, the non-verbal, presumably unintentional type, one can more clearly begin to formulate an idea of a person's self-concept. Goffman introduced many theatrical terms into the language of the dramaturgical model. For the most part one's behavior can be understood by one's routine. (Everyone has his own little song-and-dance act.) Some of the other terms he uses are:

Frontstage   You, the actor, are in the limelight; but it is the real you, and people see this, whether you are trying to conceal it or not.

Backstage   The private life of the actor, this is the preparation phase where makeup is prepared. But backstage can become frontstage for actors, and the invasion of privacy often causes suffering.

Non-Person   Those who have no access to frontstage or backstage, and so are not allowed to be part of the interaction. The old and children are in this category.

Space   This is how close or how far an actor stands to other actors.

Props   These are elements that move between encounters, but never during encounters. People get very disturbed if you change their props because these define their situation.

Equipment   These are the elements that can be manipulated in a situation.

conclusion

In outlining several prominent theorists' contributions to the formation of self-concept, we have leaned heavily toward a social psychological and sociological view of self-concept formation. It would seem to us that most practicing counselors have had a narrow exposure to self-concept. The phenomenologist view as exemplified by Rogers and by Snygg and Combs has accounted for a great deal of their theoretical exposure to self-concept and its formation. At the other end of the continuum, anyone trained or operating under a behavioral model does not deal with self-concept, which is an internalized feeling or idea one has of oneself.

We would propose using a concept of self-concept gleaned more heavily from a social-psychological point of view than has been tradition in guidance and counseling circles. While not aligning ourselves with the far extremes of Goffman's dramaturgical model of the completely situational self-identity, we would definitely borrow from Mead, who was extremely influential in formulating the early social interaction concepts of how the self is formed, and later influenced all of the symbolic interactional sociologists and most of the social psychologists and psychiatrists. Several sociological theorists, such as Howard Becker and Anselm Strauss, who are from the mainstream of the symbolic interactionist movement, affected our thinking on the direct influences of cultural and environmental concomitants on self-concept. Significant perspectives can be added from Horney's patterns of interpersonal behavior; Adler's life styles, predominately social in nature; and certainly Sullivan's theory of interpersonal relations.

However, one must admit that the construct that has been labeled self-concept originated in and was developed most fully by that school of psychology that has been variously called the "phenomenological," "perceptual," or "humanistic" approach. It is a point of view which seeks to comprehend man in the light of how he views himself. As Hamachek (1971) has stated:

> ... it is a psychology searching to understand what goes on inside
> a person in terms of how his needs, feelings, values, and unique
> ways of perceiving influence him to behave as he does.

An important underpinning of the perceptual point of view is that behavior is influenced not only by the accumulation of past and present experiences, but also, more importantly, by the personal meaning a person attaches to his perceptions of those experiences. Therefore, behavior is not simply a product of what has happened to a person from the outside, it is also a result of how he feels about himself on the inside. While it is true that a person's past experiences can have a vast influence on his present behavior, and while one cannot change what happened in the past, one can change how he feels about it today. Events cannot be changed, but perceptions about the events can be altered. Counseling, then, does not help a person in the sense of removing the problem, rather it assists an individual toward new perceptions of the problem so he can cope with it better.

It would seem to us that while the perceptual model of counseling a person toward an enhanced self-concept is useful, it also has serious limitations. It certainly has not paid enough attention to the situational aspects of forming a self-concept or to working with the social situation to enhance the person's experiences and thereby his self-concept.

The important point is, how do ideas of self get formed? Many people perceive themselves badly because of the situation in which they are placed. If a person is so situated that he constantly gets negative feedback from his interactions with significant others, then he will begin to believe that indeed he is not a very worthy person and will behave accordingly. To try counseling today's youth to alter their feelings about situations, rather than assisting them to change or control their situation, is no longer feasible or desirable. Counselors must attend more closely to the specific social and/or educational conditions that are influencing the students' negative self-image. School guidance personnel must begin to modify inappropriate and outmoded approaches as they work with youth grappling with their self-concepts in relation to the situation in which they are placed. Counselors must adhere to one of George Herbert Mead's principal tenets, that the self cannot be reconstituted without also altering the community and the social relations of the self to others within the community. The consequences of this approach to counseling and guidance work will become more apparent in later chapters as counseling approaches and counselor training strategies are discussed.

references

Adler, A. *Practice and Theory of Individual Psychology.* New York: Harcourt, Brace & World, Inc., 1927.

Angyal, A. *Foundations for a Science of Personality.* New York: Commonwealth Fund, 1941.

Augustine, St. *Confessions.* Translated by E. B. Pusey. London: Dent, 1939.

Becker, E. *The Birth and Death of Meaning.* New York: The Free Press, 1962.

Brookover, W. B.; Patterson A.; Thomas, S. *Self-Concept of Ability and School Achievement.* U. S. Office of Education, Cooperative Research Project No. 845. East Lansing: Office of Research and Publications, Michigan State University, 1962.

————."*Self-Concept of Ability and School Achievement,*" Sociology of Education 37 (1964): 271-78.

————.*Self-Concept of Ability and School Achievement, II* (Second report on the Continuing Study of Relationships of Self-Concept and Achievement. Final Report on Cooperative Research Project #1636, Improving Academic Achievement through Student's Self-Concept Enhancement.) Michigan State University College of Education Bureau of Educ. Research Service, October 1965.

Combs, A. W. "Snygg and Combs' Phenomenal Self." In *Theories of Personality,* edited by S. Hall and G. Lindzey. New York: John Wiley & Sons, Inc., 1963, p. 470.

Combs, A. W. *The Professional Education of Teachers: A Perceptual View of Teacher Preparation.* Boston: Allyn & Bacon, Inc., 1965.

Coopersmith, S. *The Antecedents of Self-Esteem.* San Francisco: W. H. Freeman and Co. Publishers, 1967.

Cooley, C. H. *Human Nature and Social Order.* New York: Charles Scribner's Sons, 1902.

Descartes, R. *Discourse on Method.* Translated by E. Anscomber and P. T. Geach. London: Nelson, 1962.

Diggory, J. C. *Self-Evaluation: Concepts and Studies.* New York: John Wiley & Sons, Inc., 1966.

Donceel, J. F. *Philosophical Psychology.* New York: Sheed & Ward, Inc., 1955.

Ford, D. H., and Urban, H. B. *Systems of Psychotherapy.* New York: John Wiley & Sons, Inc., 1963.

Freud, A. *The Ego and the Id.* London: Hogarth Press, 1950.

Freud, S. *The Standard Edition of the Complete Psychological Works of Sigmund Freud, Vol. V.* London: Hogarth Press and Institute of Psychoanalysis, 1962.

Fromm, E. "Value, Psychology, and Human Existence." In *New Knowledge in Human Values,* edited by A. H. Maslow. New York: Harper & Row, Publishers, 1959.

Goffman, E. *Presentation of Self in Everyday Life.* Garden City, New York: Doubleday & Company, Inc.

Goldstein, K. *The Organism.* New York: American Book Company, 1939.

Hall, C. S., and Lindzey, G. *Theories of Personaltiy.* New York: John Wiley & Sons, Inc., 1963.

Hamachek, D. E. *Encounters with the Self.* New York: Holt, Rinehart & Winston, Inc., 1971.

Hilgard, E. R. "Human Motives and the Concept of the Self." *American Psychologist* 4 (1949): 374-82.

Horney, Karen. *The Neurotic Personality of our Time.* New York: W. W. Norton & Company, Inc., 1937.

———. *Our Inner Conflicts.* New York: W. W. Norton & Company, Inc., 1945.

———. *Self-Analysis.* New York: W. W. Norton & Company, Inc., 1942.

James, W. *Psychology.* New York: Dover Publications, Inc., 1950.

Kinch, J. W. "A Formalized Theory of the Self." In *Symbolic Interaction: A Reader in Social Psychology,* edited by J. C. Manis and B. W. Meltzer. Boston: Allyn & Bacon, Inc., 1967.

La Benne, W. D. and Greene, B. I. *Educational Implications of Self-Concept Theory.* Pacific Palisades, California: Goodyear Publishing Company, Inc., 1969.

Lecky, P. *Self-Consistency: A Theory of Personality.* New York: Island Press, 1945.

Lewin, K. *A Dynamic Theory of Personality.* New York: McGraw-Hill Book Company, 1935.

Locke, J. *Concerning Human Understanding.* London: Oxford University Press, 1960.

Lynd, Helen M. *On Shame and the Sense of Identity.* New York: Harcourt, Brace & World, Inc., 1958.

Manis, J. G., and Meltzer, B. N. *Symbolic Interaction: A Reader in Social Psychology.* Boston: Allyn & Bacon, Inc., 1967.

Maslow, A. H. *Motivation and Personaltiy.* New York: Harper & Row, Publishers, 1954.

McCelland, D. C. *Personality.* New York: Sloane, 1951.

Mead, G. H. *Mind, Self and Society.* Chicago: University of Chicago Press, 1934.

Monroe, R. *Schools of Psychoanalytic Thought.* New York: Holt, Rinehart & Winston, 1955.

Purkey, W. W. *Self-Concept and School Achievement.* Englewood Cliffs, N. J.: Prentice-Hall, Inc., 1970.

Raimy, V. C. "The Self-Concept as a Factor in Counseling and Personality Organization." Unpublished doctoral dissertation, Ohio State University, 1943.

Rogers, C. R. *Client-Centered Therapy: Its Current Practice, Implications, and Theory.* Boston: Houghton Mifflin Company, 1951.

Rogers, C. R. "A Theory of Therapy, Personality, and Interpersonal Relationships as Developed in the Client-Centered Framework. In *Psychology: A study of a science. Vol. II. General Systematic Formulations, Learning, and Special Processes,* edited by S. Koch. New York: McGraw-Hill Book Company, 1959.

Snygg, D., and Combs, A. W. *Individual Behavior.* New York: Harper & Row, Publishers, 1949.

Sullivan, H. S. *Conceptions of Modern Psychiatry.* Washington, D.C.: William Alanson White Psychiatric Foundation, 1947.

Sullivan, H. S. *The Interpersonal Theory of Psychiatry.* New York: W. W. Norton, & Company, Inc. ,1953.

Super, D. E.; Slavishivsky, R.; Matlin, N.; Jordaan, J. P. *Career Development: Self Concept Theory.* New York: College Entrance Examination Board, 1963.

Van Steinberghen, F. *Epistemology.* Translated by Martin J. Flynn. New York: Joseph Warner, Inc., 1949.

Viney, Linda. "Self: The History of a Concept." *Journal of the History of Behavioral Sciences* 5 (1969): 349-60.

Wylie, Ruth. *Self-Concept: A Critical Survey of the Pertinent Research Literature.* Lincoln: University of Nebraska Press, 1961.

two * development of the self-concept

A person is not born with a self-concept, but forms one as a result of his experiences. He develops the capacity to view himself as an object, yet it is not deliberately taught him by his parents or others concerned with his instruction. Although a person's self-concept is of great importance, it seems to be almost a byproduct of other learning experiences. It could be said that to a great extent it is the result of incidental rather than planned learning.

the early development of a self-concept

Even in his preverbal months the young child begins to form a self-concept. With the onset of verbalization, a great deal can be learned about what a child thinks of himself by eliciting certain verbal responses from him. But, since a child begins to form his self-concept before he has learned to communicate through language, investigation of the early stages is an intricate job. Nevertheless, by observing the child's behavior closely we can begin to draw inferences about these beginning phases (Baughman and Welsh, 1962).

While still very young, a child will begin to explore his own body to satisfy curiosity about how he is put together. This exploring and testing of what the various body parts can do provides the nucleus from which the child forms a notion of his physical person and by which he establishes the boundaries that separate his physical person from the rest of the world. This early body image, as Jersild (1960) and several others have pointed out, plays a crucial part in the developing self-concept. This body image begins to form quite early but it is subject to modification — at least through adolescence. Upon attaining adulthood however, a person's body image may become more resistant to change. This conclusion is suggested, for example, by cases of adults who, having lost both legs, find it difficult to adjust their images to take account of the loss.

influence of family on a child's view of himself

Among the earliest experiences which influence the development of a person's self-concept are those with other people. The position is widely held that the child's attitudes pertaining to himself emanate from interpersonal relations with other people. The quality of these relationships determines the quality of the self-concept; first with family, then with peers in unstructured situations, then with peers and teachers in structured situations.

During his earliest years the most significant others in a child's life are his parents. Under the assumption that self-concept is learned, it would be expected that one would develop a good self-concept, without attendant anxiety, about those of his traits that are valued and rewarded by his parents, but would have a poor self-concept and marked anxiety about traits that had been punished or not rewarded (McCandless, 1961). Thus, early child-rearing practices are very important factors to consider in the self-concept formation.

Every young child has certain innate characteristics, and as far as has been determined, he originally expresses these without hesitation. Biologically, for the child to express his innate tendencies is probably a desirable experience. However, parents and others around the child do not fully accept the expression of natural tendencies; instead they tend to class his behavior as "good" or "bad" and to make value judgments about particular actions. A child frequently hears clues to parental opinions about particular actions such as "naughty, naughty," "shame on you," or "that's a good boy."

The important general principle, of course, is that a child forms his self-concept by observing the reactions of others to him. Since he has no innate value system, he is not able directly to observe himself, nor can he compare himself objectively with other children of the same age. However, he certainly can and does observe how other people react toward him and respond to him. In effect, what he observes tells him whether he is a worthy person or an unworthy person. Does he merit love, affection, warmth, or has he earned distance, ostracism and coolness? The child's mother, of course, is the most important person in this process, since she is closest to the child and interacts with him more frequently than anyone else.

Jourard and Remy (1955), in a study of body cathexes (the degree of feeling satisfaction or dissatisfaction with the various part or processes of the body), sought to determine if self-rated cathexes of body and self correlated with perceived parental view of cathexes. They found that negative parental appraisal of one's body and self was indicative of psychological insecurity. Self-appraisals vary with the person's perception or belief of parent's appraisal of his self.

Child, Frank, and Storm (1956) hypothesized that one would develop a good self-concept, without attendant anxiety, about those traits that had been valued and rewarded by parents and important others during childhood, but would have a poor self-concept and marked anxiety about traits for which one was punished or not rewarded. They asked a sample of male college students how persons important in their childhood had reacted to behaviors such as competitiveness, aggression, mannerliness, and so on. These young men also related their own self-concepts and associated anxiety in these areas. Their results gave support to their hypothesis.

In a study of the effect of parental attitudes on children's self-perceptions, Ausubel, *et al.* (1954), were able to support the hypothesis that children's self-images develop according to the pattern of parent's rewards and punishments. They concluded that when this pattern stresses objective success rather than the needs of the developing child, unfortunate characteristics may develop.

Unfortunately then, the reactions or perceived reactions of others, especially parents, often upset a young child and cause him to question his adequacy or worthiness. Mothers, because of their own problems, become quite disturbed when confronted with even a slight degree of aggression in their children. They may, therefore, try to prevent the child from acting aggressively even when the situation justifies such behavior. The way the mother handles the situation may cause the child to feel guilty if he performs in a forbidden way. The child, as a result of such experiences, may develop an unfavorable self-image.

Adults frequently respond to a child according to their own needs rather than those of the child, and in so doing fail to realize what their behavior may be doing to his self-concept. Even when parents do consider the child, often their concern reflects a conviction that the child should become the pre-conceived type of person they desire rather than to foster a feeling of self-acceptance. Conceptions of what children should be, as well as what they should become, are shaped by many forces. All parents have such conceptions and they leave their effects on the child, whether they are in line with his natural tendencies or not.

As the child leaves the early secure surroundings of the home he has definitely formed a self-concept. This self-concept is a result of the interaction and interplay of factors within his home environment. The evidence is fairly conclusive that his home environment has been an important determinant of his self-concept. At the age of two to three years, as he is able to play with other children somewhat independently of constant parental supervision, his peers begin to have important inputs into his ever-forming self-concept. For instance, if he ventures forth to play with the little boy in the next yard he finds that there are new rules to be learned. Maybe his siblings allow him certain privileges, or at least treat him with respect, but if the little boy next door tells him he is no good and refuses to play with him, the child must weigh this evidence against that already gathered. If his home situation has been positive and he has a healthy self-image, then such a brushoff is not too serious. He will go to the second or third yard over and seek a friendlier playmate. What of the child, however, whose home environment has created a rather weak self-concept? This rejection would reinforce his already forming feeling of worthlessness.

Children, then, do receive important inputs of evidence that help them perceive themselves in certain ways based on their playmates' reactions to them. It is during this time the child begins to decide if he is a fighter or peacemaker, a follower or a leader, a joiner or an initiator. These roles have been somewhat influenced by his sibling relations and will be further delineated as the child enters school.

entering school

The child's self-concept arises and develops in an interpersonal setting (Sullivan, 1947). As we have already indicated, feelings about the self are established early in life and are modified by subsequent events and experiences. Among the significant people believed to affect the child's feelings about himself are first, his parents and later, his teachers and peers. Jersild (1952) notes "that it is reasonable to assume that for many young people school is second only to the home as an institution which determines the growing individual's concept of himself and his attitudes of self-acceptance or self-rejection. Nearly all the important currents in a young person's social relationship with his peers flow through his life at school."

Much of the child's learning and perceptions about himself before he enters school have been incidental and informal for the most part. Now, however, as he enters school for the first time, the nature of this learning becomes formal and direct. The school dispenses praise and reproof, acceptance and rejection on a large-scale basis.

Unfortunately, even at the kindergarten level, schools can be hotbeds for developing negative self-concepts. Even where the school situation is almost perfect, children are likely to be reminded of their shortcomings and failures time and time again, if not by their teachers, then by their peers. Purkey (1970) says that "schools are places where students face failures, rejection, and daily reminders of their limitations. Because some schools are unable to adjust themselves to individual differences of students (in spite of their written philosophies) untold children face daily deprecation and humiliation." Yet the failures, reminders of limitations, and rejection children face in school are often artificial and forced. Though much of the failure in schools is contrived, think of the humiliating and dehabilitating effects it can have on a child's self-worth. As one looks around at many of our presently existing elementary schools, it is fairly evident that their basic *modus operandi* calls for a punitive approach to education.

Schools, hypothetically, are supported to represent the value structure of the society or the dominant community which they serve. In accordance with the prevailing atmosphere of competition as the American way of life, schools put pressures on children to compete with each other. Things are put in such a way as to communicate the message, "we will have some winners and some losers, which will you be?" Even in the earliest primary grades children begin to perceive themselves as winners or losers in competition for grades, teachers' favoritism and being liked by their peers. Purkey (1970) very aptly observes:

> Competitive evaluations, which ignore varying sociological backgrounds and individual differences in ability, often begin in the first grade and continue throughout school. "Grading on the curve" is popular, and competition among students is encouraged. Students are encouraged to enhance themselves by demonstrating their superiority over their fellow students (pp. 40-41).

Rosenberg (1965) also speaks to this point:

> No educational system in the world has so many examinations, or so emphasizes grades, as the American school system. Children are constantly being ranked and evaluated. The superior achievement of one child tends to debase the achievement of another (p. 281).

Certainly, we could concede the fact that some of the competition encouraged in our schools may come spontaneously from the children and may just reflect a healthy zest for life. However, most of the competition encouraged by schools is rather questionable. If the school is to promote healthy self-understanding and enhance positive feelings of self-worth, it will be necessary to re-assess the conceptions underlying our grade placement system and norms of achievement. Priority should be given to distinguishing, more rigorously than has been done, between competition that stems from a healthy attitude and that which is a product of anxiety and fear.

ability grouping. What are some of the effects of ability grouping on students? When students are grouped according to ability, Combs (1952) reports there is a tendency to establish and reinforce the individual's concept of his ability in a particular area, and to perpetuate it from that time. After the third year of this differential placement, the student seldom breaks from this rank. La Benne and Greene (1969) interpret these findings to mean that the child incorporates the teacher's judgment of his current status and begins to behave as expected. The child is brainwashed; he is taught a lie about himself which fixes his potentialities, and is locked in a compartment of ability.

Luchins and Luchins (1948) examined children's attitudes toward grouping. When ability groups are established within a grade, they discovered, children are not only aware of this, but strongly desire to be in the highest group. A large-scale study by

Borg (1966) investigated a number of academic and personality variables as they related to ability and random grouping for children ranked as superior, average, and slow. Borg ascertained that random grouping favored concepts of self, acceptance of self, feelings of belonging, and reduction in antisocial feelings for all ranks. While the ability grouping favored achievement scores (the elementary children ranked as superior, and those in the junior high ranked as superior and average), there was a negative relationship for all the students ranked as slow. Borg stresses that the achievement differences over a four-year period were slight. Most of the studies supporting ability grouping use achievement as the criterion measure, while most of them neglect to look at the fact that there is sufficient evidence to question ability grouping because slight gains in achievement for some students are not worth fostering negative self-concepts in others.

The authors, in their dealings with adolescents, have found that some students feel very gravely the fact that they are placed in slower or "dumb" groups based on the results of standardized tests. They were placed in these groups usually in elementary school and have never been able to overcome that stigma of being perceived by the teachers as the slower students.

grading. Another school factor that we will briefly consider is grading. Grading has become such a common practice that students and parents have been conditioned to accept it as a functional dimension of schooling. The fact that grading students is an integral part of the present educational scene, and is often seen as a most important component, makes it a plausible element in the development of the self-concept. Many times the grades assigned to the students by teachers are the only medium of communication with students. In a very real sense, teachers transmit their feelings about the students as persons via the grading experience. While it is true that teachers might provide many clues to the students during the course of a marking period, the big payoff comes on report card day. Those few numeral or letter grades that are placed on a report card often convey much more than the teacher's judgment of the student's scholastic achievement and progress.

For many reasons, the current practice and procedures of assigning grades is most unfortunate and may be very detrimental to what educators profess they are trying to accomplish. At best, grades are a rough estimate of one person's judgment. That the profession has had difficulty defining what grades really mean, or what function they perform in educating the student, should open them to serious dispute, particularly because of the inherent damage they may incur. Students can read much more into the grade the teacher assigns than the teacher meant to imply. Assigning grades does not necessarily mean that teachers are judging anything more than performance. However, if students perceive that a teacher's negative feeling is being transmitted by the assigned grade, it can be damaging to their self-concept.

the teacher and student self-evaluation. Apart from the influence the school as an institution has on a child's self-evaluation, the school also has a personal impact on each child which is dependent on the direct relations between him and his teacher. In the earlier grades the teacher is cast in the role of a parent. Later, at the high school and college levels, the teacher represents either the father or the mother figure. Jersild (1952) states: "The teacher mediates values from the culture. He is also an important factor in the interpersonal field of forces which influence the student's self-development."

Staines (1958) hypothesized that it is possible to distinguish reliably between teachers in normal classrooms by studying the frequency and kind of comment they make with reference to the self; and that it is possible to teach so that, while aiming at the normal results of teaching, specific changes can be made in the self picture. His first hypothesis was supported. Marked differences occurred between teachers in the frequency of self-reference in their comments, particularly in their positive or negative comments on the child's performance, status, and self-confidence. The second hypothesis was also supported. Statistically significant changes were found in two dimensions of the self, certainty and differentiation. Both changes were interpreted as indicative of greater psychological security.

Davidson and Long (1960) noted that it has been widely recognized that teachers influence the personality development of their students. They sought to study the important dimension of how the child perceives his teacher's feeling toward him. Specifically, they proposed to determine the relationship between children's perception of their teachers' feelings toward themselves and their self-perception, academic achievement, and classroom behavior. The results showed that a positive correlation exists between children's perception of their teachers' feelings toward them and the children's perception of themselves. This represented the first conclusive evidence that a child's self-appraisal is significantly related to his perception of the teacher's feeling toward him. Furthermore, it was shown that a positive correlation also exists between favorable perception of teachers' feelings and academic achievement and between favorable perception of teachers' feelings and desirable classroom behavior.

the adolescent self

The fact that the major task of adolescence is to forge an identity dictates that each adolescent must turn inward and assess his own self-image. In his self-inventory he asks questions like: "What am I like?" "How good am I?" "What should I or might I become?" "On what basis should I judge myself?" Rosenberg (1965) suggests three standard reasons why there is a heightened awareness of self-image during adolescence. First, late adolescence is a time of major decisions, *e.g.*, the individual must give serious thought to various occupational styles and choices. "What are my interests?" "What are my differential abilities?" "What are the advantages and disadvantages to me of specific occupations?" Other major decisions center around marriage, family, and religion, and their place in one's life. In the seventies other kinds of major decisions than those previously faced by adolescents will emerge, such as: "Shall I live in a community or a commune?"

A second reason that Rosenberg presents for a heightened awareness of self during adolescence is that it is a period of unusual and rapid gross physical changes. A boy may grow several inches taller or gain twenty pounds within a matter of months. A skinny little girl all of a sudden is a well-developed young lady. Internal physiological changes are also taking place, particularly after the onset of puberty.

Finally, adolescence is a period of unusual status ambiguity. Society does not seem to have a clear set of expectations for the adolescent. Sometimes he is treated like a child and at other times like an adult. From the adolescent's perspective he is expected to act as a responsible adult but he is not afforded any adult privileges. Thus he is unclear about his social duties and responsibilities, just as he is about his social rights and privileges.

To Rosenberg's list of reasons for the heightening of self-awareness in adolescence, we feel we must add a fourth reason, namely, the increased alienation of many of our youths. This feeling of being separated from the mainstream of American culture and some of its mores was always part of youth. There were always some youths alienated from our society. Brown (1968) speaks of these as the underachievers, the disadvantaged, the underemployed, dropouts, and delinquents. However, a series of sociologists and social psychologists began reporting over a decade ago that a whole new breed of alienated youths were beginning to emerge in Western cultures. In 1961 James S. Coleman, in his book *Adolescent Society*, detected some of the beginnings of a youth culture among adolescents who were growing very discontented and disillusioned with the existing social and political attitudes and mores of the predominant American culture. Parsons (1962) noted that American youth was in a ferment and was expressing many dissatisfactions with the current state of society. Kenniston (1961), in *The Uncommitted*, spoke more directly of this newer breed of alienated youths. Roszak (1969) clarified and discussed at length the emergence of a counterculture in America. Nevertheless, the added burdens and the pressing alienation felt by our youths is an added dimension in the counselor's attempt to aid adolescents in forging a self-concept. An already complex and difficult task of the youth counselor is becoming more complex and difficult, but ever more important because of the ensuing consequences.

factors influencing adolescent self-concept

In this section we shall examine several of the factors that influence an adolescent's self-concept. These factors are of differing importance depending on individual circumstances, and our order of presentation does not mean to convey a hierarchy of importance. Also, we must note that there will be some overlap, with some of these having interrelated effects on each other.

body image

One object that is always present in the here and now for every person is his body. Since it is always present and always in the "mind's eye," one's feeling toward his body becomes a powerful influence on his self-concept. Adolescents in particular seem to be over-conscious of their bodies and extremely sensitive about the image that body projects to the world. If we but note the fanatical adherence to style, it becomes apparent that adolescents in particular are very conscious of their body image. Hamachek (1971) gives several examples of this phenomenon: an adolescent boy overly concerned about his awkward coordination may refuse to attend dances; an adolescent girl overly sensitive to what she feels are inadequately developed breasts may be too embarrassed to date; a young man could have such a narcissistic love for his own body development that he neglects his social or intellectual growth. Certain industries have been able to induce adolescents to spend millions of dollars a year on products which are advertised as methods of improving the body's appearance. The ads further imply that the adolescent will gain hitherto unknown confidence and charm because he will feel so much better about himself.

There definitely is evidence to suggest that a person's appearance is an important determiner of self-esteem, both among males and females. Two researchers, P. F. Secord and S. M. Jourard, have carried out several studies to determine the relative effect of body size and person's feelings about himself as a person. In the first of these studies (Secord and Jourard, 1953) it was found that the feelings a person held concerning his own body closely approximated the feelings he held about himself as a person. These same researchers also asked college students to indicate the dimensions of several different parts of their anatomy, and then record their feelings of satisfaction with these dimensions. Those students who felt more accepting of and satisfied with their bodies were more likely to feel secure and confident and more likely to have higher self-esteem than those students who reported dissatisfaction with their bodies.

It would seem that each person has a fairly clear idea of how he would like to look — that is, he has a body ideal. If his body proportions come close to conforming to the dimensions and appearance of his ideal body image, he is more likely to feel good about himself and have a positive self-concept. Conversely, if there exists a great disparity a person is more likely to have a negative self-concept. It is not uncommon for a person with a poor body image to compensate for this deficit by becoming proficient in other ways, such as intellectual ability or musical talent. Another classical example of overcompensation is the small, short man who expends a lot of time and energy trying to excel in competitive sports in which height and size are a definite advantage. A study by Secord and Jourard (1953) showed that among American college males more positive body image was related to large size. In many areas of endeavor the small, short person seems to feel the need to compete more fiercely and has a strong need not just to excel but to win very decisively.

Physical appearance, then, contributes to the development of self-esteem because it helps invoke certain kinds of responses from other people. Positive feedback in the sense of people responding to our attractive appearance helps produce a healthy and positive self-concept.

parents and the adolescent self-concept

It was discussed earlier that parents, as significant others, play an influential role in the formation of a self-concept in early childhood and into the pre-adolescent years. Do the parents continue to be so pervasive an influence on the adolescent's self-concept? Generally, the answer to this question has been that parents do continue to have an influence on the emerging self-concept of their adolescent son or daughter, but that their influence is somewhat diminished compared to earlier years. However, recently Purkey (1970) expressed the view that parents' influence on their children's self-concept remains just about as strong in adolescence as it was in earlier childhood. Purkey bases his view somewhat on the evidence presented by Brookover, et al. (1965). One of Brookover's findings was that "the parents' influence (on self-perceptions) continues through the adolescent years." The subjects in Brookover's study consistently ranked parents high as "significant others," this in contradiction to the common belief that the influence of parents declines during adolescence. Purkey (1970) thus contends that parents have a more vital and continuing role in the self-perceptions of their children than has been generally recognized. Research done earlier by Silver (1958) yielded some data that would tend to support this contention. Silver asked fifty-six adolescent boys to complete self-concept rating scales from their own viewpoint and then also to rate themselves from the viewpoints of their parents and peers as they perceived them. The results indicated that the level and stability of self-concept ratings is significant by association with fathers' acceptance and to a lesser degree with mothers'. The level and stability of self-concept ratings is consistently and significantly associated with congruence between a subject's expressed self-concept and the concepts which he believed his parents had of him.

The fact that most researchers and writers see that parents, although to lesser degrees for some, still maintain an influence over adolescent self-concept, definitely has some implications for school guidance personnel. When the guidance person is attempting to work with adolescents on self-concept changes in relation to behavioral changes, parents can be utilized as powerful allies in these efforts. Parents could become powerful reinforcers of certain new behaviors.

peers and the adolescent self-concept

One of the most influential factors on an adolescent's self-concept is his peer group. The dependence of the adolescent on peer-group standards and values is markedly more slavish than that of the middle-years child (Church and Stone, 1968). The adolescent very readily turns to the peer culture and derives from it support and identity. Earlier, a research study by Silver (1958) was cited in regard to the influence that parents continue to exert upon an adolescent's self-concept. Silver also investigated the influence of peer relations on the self-concept. He found that perceived peer acceptance was just as powerful, if not more powerful, a determinant of adolescent self-concept as perceived parent acceptance. The level and stability of self-concept ratings were consistently and significantly associated with accuracy in perceiving the self as one's peers perceived it. Additionally, high and stable self-concept ratings were correlated with the subjects' private self-concept and that which they believed their peers held of them

Brim (1965), in studying the several roles that adolescents assume in forging their personality and identity, found that the peer group is influential in prescribing the behaviors the adolescent assumes not only in the role of friend and student but also in the at-home role. It was also found that one's peer group determines the criteria for popularity.

Undoubtedly the peer group is a very pervasive and strong prescriber of adolescent behavior. The adolescent's dependence on group acceptability and his need for belonging can lead to a submissive conformity to group ways. In order to guarantee acceptance and belonging, adolescents can be induced to perform acts which can produce highly injurious results. Church and Stone (1968) give a few examples that seem dated but can serve as illustrations. In the street gang, the young man or woman may have to prove himself in combat or by taking part in a violent assault on some arbitrarily chosen victim. A second illustration is the "chicken" games popular in the 1950's. One common form was to race cars directly toward each other at high speeds. The first driver to veer off was the chicken. This kind of approval seeking still exists and one of its most current manifestations is drug taking. Such games as "everyone bring a pill," have taken the place of the car chicken games. The game calls for all the pills to be put in a bowl, then everyone grabs a pill and pops it.

The dependence of adolescents on group or peer approval has become so severe that Church and Stone (1968) feel it could be labeled the "popularity neurosis." Adolescents seem to have an overwhelming need to be "popular" and bend much of their effort toward developing effective techniques for achieving this goal. Of course, the need for popularity stems in large part from the lessons parents teach their children. It is important to get along with people, to have people like you, to be well-adjusted, to listen to the voice of public opinion. It becomes especially acute in terms of the intermediate stage of the adolescent's self-image. The adolescent cannot be satisfied with what he thinks about himself; someone out there has to evaluate him and report this to him. His peer group must pass judgment on his worth in terms of what he produces — school achievement, special talents, even the physical appearance he presents.

Granted that the approval and the popularity comes from the peer group but, ironically, the adolescent's parents are not only very anxious for him to be popular but also they try to determine with whom to be popular.

This brings us to a very important point, the perennial question of who has the most influence on the adolescent's self-concept, the parents or the peers. One supposition is that, since parental influences have been long and pervasive, it is ultimately pre-eminent in adolescent decision-making. The other is that the need to conform is so great that peers hold the upper hand in this regard. Brittain (1963) states that, as they are commonly portrayed, adolescents confronted with parent-peer cross-pressures tend to opt in favor of the peer group. However, following Merton's (1957) reference group theory, Brittain explored the hypothesis that adolescent choices in response to parent-peer cross-pressures are dependent upon the character of the content alternatives presented. Brittain found that, consistent with his hypothesis, the responses of the adolescents in his study to parent-peer cross-pressures are a function of the situation. The responses reflected the adolescent's perception of peers and parents as competent guides in different areas of judgment.

While the responses obtained reflected concern to avoid being noticeably different from peers and also a concern about separation from peers, further data gathered as part of this study indicated a tendency toward parent conformity directly related to the perceived difficulty of the choices. In more difficult and long-reaching decisions, adolescents tended to turn to parents for assistance. However, some adolescents attempt to come to terms with parent-peer cross-pressure by simply not communicating with their parents.

James S. Coleman stresses quite a different point of view. For him the most pervasive influence in adolescent decision-making is peer influence. Deriving his conclusions from a study done in American high schools, Coleman emphasized that there is a distinct adolescent society in the United States. Adolescents have been separated out into institutions of their own, more or less isolated from adults' work and adults' perspectives. Adolescents remain in these institutions, treated as children, for a longer and longer period, while they are gaining social sophistication earlier and earlier.

Despite some distinct variations in the types of high schools included in Coleman's research, it was found that to varying degrees these adolescents were socially sophisticated, and their own peers were of more importance to them and their parents of less importance. An adolescent status system is established whereby rewards and punishments are dispensed to its members. The adolescent society has little material reward to dispense, so its system of rewards is reflected almost directly in the distribution of status. Thus, the peer group is the predominate and most influential force in shaping decisions for American adolescents. It seems then, that Coleman would also conclude that the adolescent's self-concept is overwhelmingly the product of peer influence and peer acceptance.

Recent sociological writings would seem to support Coleman's contention that the adolescent peer group is more influential than parents. Theodore Roszak's *Making of the Counter Culture* (1969) describes in detail a youth movement away from the technocracy which has been used to enslave rather than to free. Since most adults and parents have been enlisted or seduced into the technocracy, members of the counterculture would hardly look to them for a value structure which could serve as the basis for decision-making. Riophe (1971) speculates that the nuclear family (as it has been known) is under serious attack, especially as a cause of many of the adolescent problems that exist in today's society. Obviously if this is so, the influence of one's parents on his self-concept will be non-existent.

Thus the research available on the relative influence of the peer group versus the parental influence is inconclusive. Some of Brookover's studies (1967) have shown that parents are still significant others in the formation of self-concept. Brookover's data were gathered over several years starting in the early 1960's and it would seem that the factors promoting the demise of parental influence on self-concept at the adolescent stage of development are very prevalent today.

the self ideal

The construct of the ideal self is important in any discussion of the self-concept. If self-concept can be defined as those perceptions, beliefs, feelings, attitudes, and values which the individual views as describing himself, then the ideal self can be defined in terms of those qualities which describe the person he would like to be. Through personal and social interactions each child forms a conception of what he is; at the same time he is also forming an idea of what he should be or what he would like to be. It is quite common for parents to attempt to persuade their child to desist from behavior that is inconsistent with their ideals for him and rather to engage in behaviors that are consistent with their ideals.

In many instances parents fail to recognize the temperamental characteristics of their children and thus contribute to their alienation from their own selves by steadfastly pressuring them to become something inconsistent with their innate dispositions. Baughman and Welsh (1962) emphasize that special difficulties confront a child whose parents disagree about the ideal toward which he should strive. He may be forced to risk the displeasure of one parent to gain the approval of the other. If he is unable to handle this conflict adequately, serious anxiety can result.

Numerous studies have examined the difference between one's perceived self and his ideal self. The difference between the scores for the perceived self and the ideal self is the discrepancy score. The larger this discrepancy, the more a person is judged to be dissatisfied with himself. Additionally, persons who show a large discrepancy between the way they see themselves and the way they would like ideally to be are usually not as well-adjusted as those who are at least moderately satisfied with themselves. The existing research evidence shows that highly self-critical children and adults are more anxious, more insecure, and possibly more cynical and depressed than self-accepting persons (McCandless, 1961, p. 193).

Havighurst (1946) and his colleagues studied the growth of the ideal self during childhood and adolescence by asking boys and girls to write a brief essay on "The Person I Would Like to Be." A content analysis of this data disclosed that there is a developmental trend in the formation of the ideal self. The ideal self begins in childhood, usually by identifying with a parental figure. Parents or parent age models begin to fade as important for the child between ages 8 and 10. During middle childhood and into early adolescence the ideal self undergoes a romantic and glamorous phase. Glamorous idols, such as movie and sports figures, are very prominent in determining the ideal self between ages 10 and 15. Finally, late adolescents crystallize the ideal self as a composite of desirable characteristics which may be symbolized by a visible and known young adult or possibly an imaginary figure.

The environment in which the person grows up has a definite effect upon his ideal self, just as it does upon his perceived self. Havighurst and Taba (1949), while cautioning against overgeneralization, did find that young people from families of lower economic status, as a group lag behind those of middle socioeconomic status in progressing through the development stages outlined above.

maintenance of the self-concept

Changes in self-concept are required by the process of maturing. However, when an individual is still in the process of making new discoveries about his attributes and potentials as a person, he has a strong tendency to cling to already formed concepts or attitudes about himself. Lecky (1945) described this as a striving toward self-consistency; that is, a person's behavior expresses an effort to maintain the integrity, unity, and inner consistency of the personality system which has as its basis the individual's evaluation of himself. Thus, while the self is continuously growing and changing, it also paradoxically seeks to prevent growth and change.

the self and its defenses

In order to effect this preservation of one's self-concept, a person can begin to build a sophisticated array of defense mechanisms. Every person adopts certain favorite defense mechanisms which he calls into use at various times when the self is threatened or when he anticipates a threatening situation. The defense mechanisms are the learned adjustive behaviors which involve a certain amount of reality distortion and self-deception. A person's defense mechanisms help him to adjust to situations which cause conflict and frustration, and because they guard his self-concept, they function to protect the self against more serious disturbances. Thus, defense mechanisms are not only quite necessary, but also useful and desirable, except when they are used to excessive degrees and so operate at the expense of a person's ultimate adaptive efficiency and his progression toward greater maturity.

Although defense mechanisms are a necessity, they can prove to be debilitating if a person uses his defense mechanisms to avoid assuming responsibility, making decisions, or testing reality. Often a person may use defense mechanisms to help manufacture excuses for persisting in behaviors which may be immature or counterproductive to his stated goals. For the most part, we must stress that a person's use of defense mechanisms is a very normal human reaction. It is only when these defenses are used to an extreme and begin to interfere with the maintenance of self-esteem rather than aid it that they become debilitating.

Defense mechanisms generally fall into two categories, the primary defense processes and the secondary defense adjustments (White, 1964). The primary defense processes include repression and denial of reality. Regression, projection, reaction formation, and rationalization are the major secondary defense adjustments.

the primary defense process

The primary defense process is inhibition, which is a constant and indispensable feature of all ordinary activity in the nervous system. Even such relatively simple acts as walking cannot be performed without synchronized inhibitions of certain muscle groups. Defensive inhibition is no different in principle from what goes on all the time; it is simply an intense, indiscriminate inhibitory response produced by a serious threat. However, under certain conditions of mounting anxiety a person's behavior progressively loses its inhibitory controls and becomes disorganized and indiscriminate. Defensive inhibition is not a discriminating response to a threatening situation; it is a desperate and primitive response.

repression. In her book on defense mechanisms, Anna Freud (1937) allots a special status to repression. She emphasizes the point that other defenses are very often combined with repression, and she entertains the possibility that "other methods have only to complete what repression has left undone" (52).

There is something about repression that differentiates it from the other defense mechanisms. It is more fundamental, more drastic, more primitive than the other defense mechanisms. White (1964) stresses this point:

> Repression . . . is to be conceived as a direct manifestation of what we have discerned to be the basic protective device: defense inhibition (p. 212).

Repression, along with denial, is classified as the primary defense process. The other defense mechanisms are seen as secondary processes serving to fortify the primary defenses and adjust the person to its consequences.

Repression is a primitive device for dealing with impulses that seem to threaten one's psychological security (self-concept). In effect, one tries to do away with a wish or desire by refusing to acknowledge its presence. This is done because it would be inconsistent with the self-concept. When an impulse is repressed, it is pushed out of consciousness and an attempt is made to proceed as if the impulse did not exist. However, an impulse does not cease to exist even when repressed, but rather constantly seeks an outlet. The result is that the person must expend energy in order to maintain the repression. The repression of undesirable impulses and experiences not only demands considerable energy, but it also hinders healthy personality growth. A more realistic confrontation of problems is always more conducive to good mental health and positive self-development.

denial. A person can remove a threat to the self-concept simply by denying its existence. When a person cannot escape or attack a threat, the only bearable alternative may be to deny it.

There are two distinct varieties of denial, one using fantasy, the other using words and acts. Denial as fantasy could be demonstrated in the case of a withdrawn child who imagines that he

rationalization

owns a tame lion which he can easily control but which frightens other people. This fantasy is of great importance to the child and carries through endless variations, and the lion becomes the child's constant companion. Denial in word and act are demonstrated for us several times each day in our own behavior as well as that of others. We turn away from unpleasant sights; we refuse to talk about unpleasant topics; we ignore or disclaim criticism. It is quite common for a vain person to deny his impaired vision by refusing to wear eyeglasses or for an older person to deny a hearing loss rather than to wear a hearing aid.

The defense mechanism of denial can guard against discomfiting or even painful experiences. However, these simple mechanisms of denial remain available only as long as a person can tolerate the existence of a play and pretend world. Once serious reality-testing takes place, real facts can no longer be denied in the interest of everyday defense. Then progress toward more effective living and greater maturity of self can be facilitiated.

It must be remembered that denial is a part of the primary defensive process. So, in times of acute emergencies, when reality-testing becomes too overpowering and breaks down the defenses, regression to the basic unadorned process of denial might occur. Everything is inhibited which might tell him of the presence of a threat to his self-concept.

secondary defensive adjustments

A careful study of the other defense mechanisms will reveal that they quite regularly presuppose an element of repression or denial. That is, they consist of defensive inhibition followed by secondary adjustments that serve to strengthen the inhibition and bring the person to terms with it. These secondary adjustments are part of the repertoire of normal behavior. They become defense mechanisms only through their linkage with defensive inhibition, which causes them to have the characteristics of excess and rigidity.

Several different authors have compiled several different sets of defense mechanisms which we have classified as being secondary defensive adjustments. Rather than discussing all of these possible defense mechanisms, we have chosen to look briefly at what we consider to be the four major secondary defensive adjustments. These are projection, reaction formation, rationalization, and regression.

projection. Projection is usually defined as the attribution of one's own thoughts, feelings, and impulses to other persons or objects in the outside world. Its basis lies in the fact that our own feelings tend to influence our perception of the world. The defense mechanism of projection has two stages: (a) failure to recognize a characteristic in one's own self, and (2) attributing this characteristic to another person who does not actually possess it. An example is the tightfisted individual who fails to recognize his own stinginess, but quickly attributes the trait to others who are actually more generous than he. Such an individual is attempting to rid himself of an undesirable attribute by casting it onto others. This is done, of course, without conscious intent. It is an example of what is described as simple projection.

The process, however, can be more complicated. An impulse or attribute may be changed into its opposite before being projected. For example, if a man had strong erotic impulses toward other males, he probably would repress them because he cannot accept them. Not only does he repress these impulses, but he may also develop a feeling of hatred toward the objects of his affections. But since hate is also an unacceptable emotion, he may also project that and perceive others as hating him. So "I love him" becomes "he hates me."

Such projections help maintain one's feeling of adequacy and self-esteem in the face of failure. Often they are attempts to cleanse oneself of an undesirable attribute, but they can become a means of bolstering one's own position by downgrading that of another.

reaction formation. The mechanism of reaction formation involves the development of tendencies or traits that are the very opposite of those tendencies we do not like in ourselves. An example of this would be a man who suddenly realizes he is very dependent and because he is ashamed of this resolves to be scrupulously self-sufficient in everything. He then becomes independent almost to a fault, but it does not reach the proportions of desperate defense.

Reaction formation has adjustive value insofar as it helps us maintain socially approved behavior and to control unacceptable impulses. Normal development often proceeds in just this way. Suppose, however, that the reaction formation is preceded by defensive inhibition. This defense mechanism can then become self-deceptive and can lead to exaggerated and rigid fears or beliefs which could lead to excessive harshness or severity in dealing with the values of others and ourselves (Hamachek, 1971).

rationalization. The characteristics of rationalization are widely recognized. When we say a person is rationalizing, we mean that he is offering an explanation for his behavior, or what happened to him. This explanation is not correct and is meant to hide or disguise the true reason. Usually in such an event a person offers an explanation that he figures will be more palatable than the real reason. For example, Bob may rationalize that he was cut from the basketball team because he was not tall enough, whereas in fact several other boys of similar height had been chosen. The rationalization helps maintain his self-esteem.

Sometimes a person will rationalize without recognizing that he is doing so; at other times he could be quite aware of what he is doing. Not infrequently a person may rationalize and only later realize what he has done. For some persons, such a delayed recognition may lead to guilt feelings because they have "lied."

Hamachek (1971) notes that it is difficult to know where an objective consideration of facts leaves off and rationalization begins. He offers two behavioral symptoms of excessive rationalization: (1) hunting for reasons to justify belief or behavior, and (2) getting emotional (angry, guarded, up-tight) when someone questions your motives.

stability of the self-concept

Earlier in this chapter it was noted that self-concepts are very much influenced by significant others and our perception of how significant others feel and think about us. It was also noted that first parents, then siblings and peers, later teachers and classmates have a substantial influence on one's view of himself. It seems then that self-concept begins to form very early in life and throughout the growing-up period is subjected to many influences that may change or alter it. An important question to consider in examining adolescent self-concepts is how stable is a self-concept. If it has a pervasive influence over adolescent behavior, just how constant and persistent an influence can one's self-concept be if it is very unstable? Is it unstable throughout childhood and adolescence, becoming stable in adulthood? At what age does it become relatively stable?

Engels (1959), in a study on the self-concepts of adolescents, incorporated longitudinal data to determine the stability of self-concept over a two-year period. Concurrently, she also sought to determine the relationship between whatever stability she found and the quality of the self-concept. The inter-relationships between self-concept and stability, quality of the self-concept, and several indices of adjustment were also examined. Her findings indicated that there was a relative stability over a two-year period for the 107 adolescents in her study. About one-half of the subjects were in the eighth and the other one-half were in the tenth grade when the research began. Subjects whose self-concepts were negative at the first testing were significantly less stable in self-concept than the subjects whose self-concept was positive. Those adolescents who persisted in negative self-concepts over a two-year period gave evidence of significantly more maladjustment than subjects with a positive self-concept.

A more recent study conducted by Carlson (1965) investigated the changes in the structure of the self-image of 49 students studied first as sixth graders and then as high-school seniors. Despite their differences in methodology, Carlson's findings with regard to self-esteem are consistent with Engels (1959) results, suggesting that self-esteem is a relatively stable dimension of personality and one which is independent of sex role.

The studies carried out by Engels (1959) and Carlson (1965), and the few other investigations into the stability of the self-concept over time, were conducted under what could generally be called "normal conditions." However, before counselors begin to explore with someone the possible meaning of their expressed self-concept, we should assess under what conditions or in what kind of situation he is operating. If a person is under considerable pressure, he may perceive himself quite differently than he would ordinarily. Baughman and Welsh (1962) point out, for example, the phenomenon observed at the international espionage trials, where individuals have been brought to describe themselves according to their captors' demands, even though the descriptions may not necessarily agree with what they would say when not under duress.

Two of the empirical studies available that have studied the stability of self-concept involved college students and, interestingly, the results showed that under stressful situations more positive self-concepts were expressed rather than more negative self-concepts, as in the above-mentioned espionage trials. The first of these done by Abernathy (1954) involved college girls who were rushing for a sorority. A self-inventory was administered first under conditions that seemed to guarantee anonymity, although each person's inventory could be identified. Then a second administration was given in which it was made clear that the results would be examined by the sorority leaders. On the second administration forty-two out of fifty girls presented a more positive and more favorable self-concept, only five a less favorable one.

In the other study carried out by Levanway (1955), thirty college students described themselves and five other persons by use of rating scales. The subjects' attitudes towards others were also measured by a specially designed picture sorting test. In later individual testing sessions, the students repeated these tasks shortly after having been told their behavior was indicative of someone with serious emotional conflict. Substantially more positive scores for both self and others were recorded on the second administration. Unfortunately, Levanway does not report the use of a control group, so it can not be said for certain that these more positive scores would not have occurred on the second trial, even if the stressful information about a suspected emotional conflict had not been given.

Thus, based on the sparse research available on stability of the self-concept, it could be concluded that there is a relatively high degree of stability carrying through the pre-adolescent period and into the adolescent period. However, there are certain periods when a person may be placed under undue tension and this can temporarily cause an unstable and unexpected reaction. Additionally, the self-concepts of individuals operating in tension-filled situations may be affected. The counselor must be aware of these temporary, or sometimes long-term, circumstances, and must assist the individual in these trying times.

references

Abernathy, Ethel. "The Effect of Sorority Pressures on the Results of a Self-Inventory." *Journal of Social Psychology* 40 (1954): 177-83.

Ausubel, D. P.; Balthazar, E. E.; Rosenthal, Irene; Blackman. L. S.; Schpoont, S. H.; Welhowtz, Joan. "Perceived Parent Attitudes as Determinants of Children's Ego Structure." *Child Development* 25 (1954): 173-83.

Baughman, E. E., and Welsh, G. S. *Personality: A Behavioral Science.* Englewood Cliffs, N. J.: Prentice-Hall, Inc., 1962.

Carlson, Rae. "Stability and Change in the Adolescent's Self-Image." *Child Development* 36 (1965): 659-66.

Child, I. L.; Frank, Kitty F.; Storm, T. "Self-Ratings and TAT: Their Relation to Each Other and to Childhood Background." *Journal of Personality* 25 (1956): 96-114.

Cohen, J. "An Aid in the Computation of Correlation Based on Q Sorts." *Psychology Bulletin* 54, (1957): 138-39.

Dahlstron, W. G., and Welsh, G. S. *A MMPI Handbook: A Guide to Use in Clinical Practice and Research.* Minneapolis: University of Minnesota Press, 1960.

Davidson, H. H., and Lang, G. "Children's Perceptions of Their Teachers' Feelings Toward Them Related to Self Perception, School Achievement and Behavior." *Journal of Experimental Education* 29 (1960): 107-118.

Edwards, A. L. *The Social Desirability in Personality Assessment and Research*. New York: Holt, Rinehart & Winston, Inc., 1957.

Engel, Mary. "The Stability of the Self-Concept in Adolescence." *Journal of Abnormal and Social Psychology* 58 (1959): 211-15.

Freud, Anna. *The Ego and the Mechanisms of Defense*. London: Hogarth Press, Ltd., 1937.

Hamachek, D. E., ed. *The Self in Growth, Teaching and Learning*. Englewood Cliffs, N. J.: Prentice-Hall, Inc. 1965.

_____.*Encounters with the Self*. New York: Holt, Rinehart & Winston, Inc., 1971.

Havighurst, R. J.; Robinson, Myra Z.; Dorr, Mildred. "The Development of the Ideal Self in Childhood and Adolescence." *Journal of Educational Research* 40 (1946): 241-57.

Havighurst, R. J., and Taba, Hilda. *Adolescent Character and Personality*. New York: John Wiley & Sons, Inc., 1949.

Jersild, A. T. *In Search of Self*. New York: Bureau of Publications, Teachers College, Columbia University, 1952.

_____.*Child Psychology*. Englewood Cliffs, N. J.: Prentice-Hall, Inc., 1960.

Jourard, S. M., and Remy, R. M. "Perceived Parental Attitudes, the Self and Security." *Journal of Consulting Psychology* 19 (1955): 364-66.

La Benne, W. D., and Greene, B. I. *Educational Implications of Self-Concept Theory*. Pacific Palisades, California: Goodyear Publishing Company, Inc., 1969.

Lecky, P. *Self-Consistency: A Theory of Personality*. New York: Island Press, 1945.

Levanway, R. W. "The Effect of Stress on Expressed Attitudes toward Self and Others. *Journal of Abnormal and Social Psychology* 50 (1955): 225- 26.

McCandless, B. R. *Children and Adolescents*. New York: Holt, Rinehart & Winston, Inc., 1961.

Osgood, C. E.; Suci, G. J.; Tannebaum, P. H. *The Measurement of Meaning*. Urbana: University of Illinois Press, 1951.

Purkey, W. W. *Self-Concept and School Achievement*. Englewood Cliffs, N. J.: Prentice-Hall, Inc., 1970.

Rosenberg, M. *Society and the Adolescent Self-Image*. Princeton, N. J.: Princeton University Press, 1965.

Sheldon, W. H. *The Varieties of Human Physique*. New York: Harper and Brothers, 1940.

_____. *The Varieties of Temperament*. New York: Harper and Brothers, 1942.

Staines, J. W. "The Self-Picture as a Factor in the Classroom."*British Journal of Educational Psychology* 28 (1958): 97-111.

Stephenson, W. *The Study of Behavior: Q-Technique and its Methodology.* Chicago: University of Chicago Press, 1953.

Sullivan, H. S. *Conceptions of Modern Psychiatry.* Washington, D. C.: William Alanson White Psychiatric Foundation, 1947.

Washburn, W. C. "The Effects of Physique and Intrafamily Tension on Self-Concepts in Adolescent Males." *Journal of Consulting Psychology* 26 (1962): 460-66.

White, R. W. *The Abnormal Personality*, 3rd ed. New York: The Ronald Press, 1964.

Wylie, Ruth. *Self-Concept: A Critical Survey of the Pertinent Research Literature.* Lincoln: University of Nebraska Press, 1961.

three * self-concept and behavior

If we accept the assumption that one behaves as one perceives, we would rightly expect that certain behaviors of a youth are determined by what he believes about himself and what worth he has learned to place on himself. These behaviors, of course, could be either positive and enhancing, or negative and debilitating.

Counselors assist persons with positive self-concepts to further enhance their feelings of self-worth and help them expand their self-awareness. Counselors assist these persons toward personal growth and greater development as human beings and then lead them to become helpers and facilitators themselves. However, most of the people who seek a counselor have more negative than positive feelings about themselves at the time they seek counseling. This section will discuss behaviors or patterns of behaving which are related to an individual's self-concept.

self-concept and anxiety

Anxiety is the state of being threatened, a vague feeling of fear from an unknown source. Anxiety is different from fear, in that with fear the person knows what it is that threatens him. When he experiences anxiety or fear, he has an innate physiological reaction (heart pounding faster, hands perspiring and trembling, nervousness, etc.). Self-concept involves everything concerning the self: how a person sees himself, his values, goals, strengths, and weaknesses; how he thinks, feels, and acts; all are part of his sense of self. Self-esteem refers more to an individual's personal judgments of worthiness or unworthiness, approval or disapproval that are expressed in the attitudes he holds toward himself.

figure 1

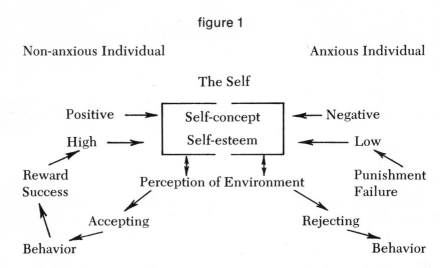

Non-anxious Individual   Anxious Individual

The Self

Positive ⟶ Self-concept ⟵ Negative

High ⟶ Self-esteem ⟵ Low

Reward
Success   Perception of Environment   Punishment
Failure

Accepting   Rejecting

Behavior   Behavior

From infancy each individual gains a picture of himself through interacting with others. From his vantage point he perceives the environment that surrounds him, which may be either accepting or rejecting. Through past experiences he has developed needs and defined goals. In striving to meet these needs and to reach his goals, he emits certain behaviors for which he is rewarded or punished, thereby enhancing, damaging, or reinforcing the prevailing self-concept. Figure 1 indicates that there are two possible directions or kinds of interaction: one of an anxious person, and one of a non-anxious person, both forming generally repetitious cycles unless one of the factors given is somehow changed.

Individuals see themselves in generally positive or negative ways. As a result of their past experiences, they come to define themselves: in the case of negative self-perception, as unworthy, unwanted, unacceptable, and unable (Snygg and Combs, 1949).

Consequently they have a low self-esteem. An individual with low self-esteem is more likely than others to experience the various physiological indicators of anxiety, such as hand trembling, nervousness, insomnia, heart pounding, pressure in the ear, fingernail biting, etc. (Rosenberg, 1965). For every one of the indicators of anxiety cited by Rosenberg and by Fromm-Reichmann (1960), people low in self-esteem were conspicuously more likely than those with high esteem to report having had such experiences.

Referring again to Figure 1, one can see that the individual with a positive self-concept would experience "normal" (Horney talks about "normal" anxiety such as that concerning death, etc.) or little anxiety. However, the individual with a negative self-concept would exhibit high anxiety, both cycles being self-reinforcing. For example, the individual having a negative self-concept and high anxiety would perceive his environment as rejecting (which may be what causes his negative self-concept), and in striving to meet his particular needs and goals, he would act in certain ways. A person with high anxiety and negative self-concept may develop inappropriate behavior to cope with such feelings. His behavior, therefore, will be punished, or he may experience failure which would reinforce the way he already feels about himself. He perceives himself as being no good, a failure, unworthy, and unaccepted.

The path is the same for the individual with a positive self-concept — only in the opposite direction. Although these cycles are self-reinforcing, it is possible to change the direction or switch cycles of the anxious or non-anxious person by changing either the perception of self, the environment, the behavior, or the rewards and punishments.

The circular effect seems to apply to self-concept and anxiety. Horney considers anxiety to be of central significance and she sees anxiety as the catalyst that sets in motion a complex chain of psychological events which produce, among other things, self-hatred and self-contempt: a negative self-concept. According to Horney, then, anxiety tends to generate low self-esteem. However, the opposite sequence can occur where low self-esteem may generate anxiety.

Rosenberg (1965) and Coopersmith (1967) feel that low self-esteem creates anxiety. Their research reveals certain factors associated with low self-esteem which may be expected to create anxiety. The first of these factors is stability of self-image. People with low self-esteem experience an inordinate amount of anxiety because of shifting and unsettled self-images. The single most important point of reference in evaluting new experiences or stimuli is one's self-image. If a person has unclear and shifting opinions, attitudes, and perceptions of himself, then he is deprived of his most important frame of reference, and he is prone to be anxious.

Another factor that seems to contribute to the association between low self-esteem and anxiety is the tendency of people with low self-esteem to present themselves under a guise or a false front. This false front is essentially a coping mechanism used to overcome the feeling of worthlessness by convincing others that one is worthy. Putting on this facade is anxiety-producing because it is a constant strain. By sheer force of will to act cheerful when one is angry, or sympathetic when one is really indifferent, is very fatiguing. A second source of tension comes from the threat of making a false move and thereby revealing some inconsistency or destroying the facade. Rosenberg (1965) showed that, among adolescents, those with low self-esteem have a high tendency to put on false fronts.

Yet a third source which contributes to high anxiety among those with low self-esteem is that these people are extraordinarily sensitive to any evidence in their daily life which could suggest inadequacy. Horney (1950) called this tendency vulnerability. That those with low self-esteem are very vulnerable is demonstrated by the sensitivity they display toward criticism. They also exhibit deep disturbance when laughed at, scolded, or blamed. Additionally, they are likely to be deeply concerned about poor performance of any undertaken task, they are very disturbed when any inadequacy in themselves is revealed, and they are very prone to be "touchy and easily hurt" (Rosenberg, 1965).

anxiety is learned. From the consequences of his interaction with the environment, an individual learns cues which become anxiety-provoking. Anxiety restricts our perceptions, thereby distorting reality. The individual tends to misjudge cues in his environment. In striving to meet his needs and to reach his goals his behavior becomes inappropriate. Through rewards and/or punishments, situations become threatening or non-threatening.

For many individuals, school becomes a threatening situation producing anxiety. Kaplon (1970) discusses anxiety arising from the school situation as a result of what is valued by the child and/or his parents. If the general atmosphere of the child is not concerned with scholastic success, this is for him a usual state of affairs and no psychological conflict arises. A child in this situation seldom experiences anxiety because of fear of failure, and his time is used developing social ways of behaving. When anxiety erupts in this child, it is from the social scene. The event of grade retention is often traumatic, but only as it results in the loss of prestige in the peer group. Once he finds he can relate to his new peer group, the child's anxiety lessens. Children can experience anxiety from loss of praise by teachers or peers, and can gradually turn to hostile aggression if they do not receive praise. This hostile state is the rejection of the reality demands of the moment to maintain his self-esteem, and a way to deal with the anxiety because of failure in the social sphere. Frequent punishment by the teacher reinforces the child's image of a rejecting environment. This will eventually lead to dropping out or expulsion. An accepting class atmosphere would reduce anxiety and in effect reinforce behavior that will enable children to gain social success.

If the child comes from an environment in which scholastic success is valued, failure in school will bring about a sense of personal failure. Anxiety here is the response to possible rejection and parent disapproval. This child cannot reject the environment, since this will be a rejection of himself and a devaluation of self. Such anxiety may produce a feeling that the child does not like himself and that others do not like him, either. If he feels this way he may try *not* to succeed. As he acts out, punishment will reinforce his negative self-concept. He may be afraid to take a chance in learning because he may fail. The teacher can help by making his standards attainable, and reducing the child's internal standards, and enhancing his self-esteem.

self-concept and school

Throughout this text it has been stressed that a positive feeling toward self emanating from a healthy understanding and acceptance of self is a major key to mental health; the healthy individual is one who understands and accepts himself. The concept of self has been ascribed a key role as a factor in the interpretation of personality, in motivating behavior, and in achieving mental health. Thus the nurture and fostering of a positive self-concept becomes an important task for education. Phillips (1960) contends that for many young children the school is second only to the home as an institution which determines the growing individual's concept of himself and his attitudes toward self-acceptance or self-rejection.

There is ample evidence in the research literature to show that, indeed, the school plays an enormous part in the development of one's self-concept and behavior. A low or negative self-concept can have adverse effects on a child's school performance even at an early age. Wattenberg and Clifford (1964) detected that many children have already acquired an unfavorable view of themselves and poor achievement is established before they enter the first grade. Such early established attitudes can have detrimental effects on the entire school career of a person. Many years ago Lecky (1945) pointed out how low academic achievement may be related to a person's conception of himself as being unable to learn academic material. Lecky observed, for instance, that some children make the same number of errors in spelling per page no matter how difficult or easy the material. These children spelled as if there were a built-in upper limit to their ability. Lecky devised a theory built around the construct of self-consistency to which he related school performance as well as other areas of human functioning. When certain patterns of behavior are established, it is very hard to break these patterns even if they are negative and detrimental; i.e., people act consistently.

Educators have been calling attention to the high positive correlation between healthy enhancing concepts of self and high achievement levels in school. At the opposite pole, it is easily seen that negative self-concept and low achievement also have a high positive correlation. Purkey (1970) states that academic success or failure appear to be as deeply rooted in concepts of the self as it is in measured ability, if not deeper. Brookover (1965) concluded, based on longitudinal research on self-image and achievement, that the assumption that human ability is the most important factor in achievement is questionable, and that the student's attitudes limit the level of achievement in school. La Benne and Greene (1969) caution very strongly against the idea that I.Q. is a satisfactory measure of a person's intrinsic intellectual ability. They, like Brookover, feel that if a person has a faulty perception of his abilities based on a faulty perception of himself, there will be a serious blockage created which will prove detrimental to his level of achievement in school.

It is very interesting, but at the same time frightening, to speculate upon why individuals in our society are prone to have negative feelings about themselves, if not generally, then at least in one of several specific aspects of their lives. How many people go through life functioning at levels very much or somewhat below the level they could function because somehow they have come to believe that they are only capable of a low level? What role does the school play in creating and then reinforcing these negative self-concepts and later perpetuating them? The school counselor particularly must wonder about this, since so many of the students crossing his portal do so because of low grades or other academic difficulties which stem from negative attitudes such as "I knew I couldn't do it anyhow" or feedback such as "the teacher said that I was not smart enough to be in his class."

In 1961 Ruth Wylie produced a scholarly and monumental work entitled *The Self-Concept: A Critical Survey of Pertinent Research Literature.* Wylie reviewed comprehensively the studies that had been produced in research projects up to 1959: theses, dissertations, and many journal articles concerned with the self-concept. We will comment on some research produced "post Wylie."

Since 1960 there has been a noticeable increase in research on the self-concept. At the time Wylie published her book she was optimistic about the possibilities of research into the self-concept but pessimistic about the research efforts up to that time. It was partially because of Wylie's milestone work, but also because of improved methodology and research design technology, that it is generally agreed that research has improved and moved ahead in this area. One facet of this research that has received much attention from psychologists and educators is the persistent and significant relationship between self-concept and academic achievement (Purkey, 1970).

It was already noted previously that Wattenberg and Clifford (1964) found, through a study of kindergarten children's self-attitudes and their subsequent school achievement, that an unfavorable view of self and poor achievement is already established in many children before they enter the first grade. When a child starts out with a negative feeling about his ability to do well in school, it would be expected that he would achieve poorly in his early school years. Does this relationship of poor self-concept and poor school achievement continue into the later school years?

Several studies on achievement and self-concept have been carried out by Melvin C. Shaw and his co-workers. In one of these (Shaw and McCuen, 1960) the researchers investigated whether there would be a continuance of low achievement and negative self-concept. They hypothesized that there would be, based on their previous observations and on the premise that academic underachievement is related to basic personality structure. They studied a group of eleventh- and twelfth-graders who had been in the same school district since the first grade. Those of this category scoring in the upper quartile of intelligence tests administered at the eighth-grade level were divided into achiever and underachiever groups and further into male and female groups: thus, there were four basic groups: male achievers (N=36), male underachievers (N=36), female achievers (N=45), and female underachievers (N=17). The results revealed that, for boys, underachievement can begin as early as the first grade, is definitely present by the third grade, and becomes increasingly more serious in the high-school years. For girls, the problem may exist as early as the sixth grade, and is definitely present and of increasing importance from the ninth to the eleventh grades.

There have been several other research efforts to link self-concept and achievement through study of the phenomenon of underachievement. In an investigation by Shaw, *et al.* (1960), involving bright underachieving high-school students, it was found that female underachievers feel relatively more positive about themselves than do male underachievers. No simple generalization was warranted for the girls except that the female underachievers in this study had ambivalent feelings about themselves. A later study by Shaw and Alves (1963) confirmed the findings of the earlier study by indicating again that female underachievers have more positive feelings about themselves than do the males. In this same study, however, a trend did emerge which showed that male and female underachievers have generally different perceptual modes. The negative perceptual self-feeling of male underachievers appears to revolve primarily around themselves, while the negative attitudes of the female underachievers were centered more on the perceptions of themselves by others.

That there are sex differences in the way underachievers perceive themselves has been noted by several other researchers. Both Campbell (1966) and Bledsoe (1967) found a stronger relationship between self-concept and achievement in boys than in girls. Male underachievers tend more toward negative self-concepts than female underachievers. Fink (1962), in a study of the relationship between academic achievement and self-concept, found significant differences between achievers and underachievers. He also found there is a strong tendency in underachieving boys to have lower self-perceptions than do underachieving girls. Borislaw (1962), drawing his sample from a population quite different from Fink's, investigated the importance of self-evaluation as a non-intellective factor in scholastic achievement. Borislaw did his study with 197 college freshmen as his subjects. Combs (1963), in examining the relationship between self-perception and achievement in high-school boys, determined that underachievers see themselves as less adequate and less acceptable to others, and they find their peers and adults less acceptable. Hogan and Green (1971) determined that one's self-concept is directly linked to school achievement, and that teachers of ghetto children particularly must begin attending to this.

A series of extensive research projects carried out longitudinally over several years (1962-68) by Brookover and his associates reported self-concept of scholastic ability and school achievement are significantly related for both boys and girls. This relationship persists even when intelligence is factored out. Brookover and his colleagues were looking at a specific kind of self-concept, namely self-concept of ability, rather than global self-concept. Thus their findings showed achievement in school to be limited by the student's concept of his ability. Additionally, they found that self-concept of ability is a better predictor of success in school than overall self-concept.

The above-mentioned studies do not in any manner exhaust the number of studies we could go on citing to point out that successful students usually have a positive and healthy self-concept, while it is likely that those who are achieving poorly in school have a negative self-concept.

Inevitably when there is a discussion concerning the relationship between self-concept and achievement the question arises as to which comes first, a positive self-concept or high achievement. Hamachek (1971) feels it is not possible to give a definitive answer to this question. While it is not possible to say with precision which comes first, good work or positive self-concept, it seems reasonable and logical to conclude that each is mutually reinforcing to the extent that a positive change in one facilitates a positive change in the other. In the final analysis we must seek the answer in each individual case by review and diagnosis of the circumstances. It would seem very plausible, however, that if school were a happy place where every person could experience success according to his individual needs and ability, then teachers and counselors would encounter fewer and fewer incidents of morbid, self-defeating perceptions and attitudes in young persons.

self-concepts in vocational development

An area of behavior where one's self-perception becomes manifest is the choice of occupations, or the planning that leads eventually to a vocational choice. In the field of vocational psychology there has been much activity devoted to studying the linkage between one's self-concept, vocational interests, and the type of career finally embarked upon. Much of this activity has been influenced by the theoretical formulations of Donald E. Super. According to Super (1951), a person, in expressing a vocational preference, puts into occupational terminology his ideas of the kind of person he is; in entering an occupation, he seeks to implement a concept of himself; in getting established in an occupation he achieves self-actualization. In this way the occupation makes possible the playing of a role appropriate to one's self-concept.

Super (1963) remarks on the fact that there has been a lack of communications between the personality, social, and clinical psychologists and their colleagues, the counseling psychologists — and maybe we should add to Super's list the school counselors and others in education. The several reviews of the literature on self-concept do not include any of the literature on the self-concept and vocational development. Even Wrenn's (1958) review of the literature on the self-concept in counseling does not mention the topic of vocational choice and adjustment nor does it include anything on self-concepts in vocational development. Strong and Feder's (1961) review of the measurement of self-concept also neglects the subject. Wylie's (1961) very scholarly review of self-concept research also neglected to include the research on self-concept and vocational development.

self-concept and vocational choice. Donald Super and his associates have been the chief proponents of what Osipow (1968) has called a "Developmental Self-Concept Theory of Vocational Behavior." Super's theoretical framework is based on three psychological areas — differential psychology, self theory, and developmental psychology. Despite considerable production through the Career Pattern Study, Super's theory remained rather general for about ten years (1953-63). But 1963 the publication *Career Development: Self-Concept Theory* appeared and provided more explicit and detailed accounting of how vocational development should occur. In this monograph Super explicitly defined the notion of self-concept and its various aspects. From there he worked into the construct of vocational self-concept, which is the system of major concern for Super.

Just as the general self-concept of each person is continuously developing and shifting through life as experiences indicate that shifts are necessary to reflect reality, so too the vocational self-concept shifts and changes. As one matures, he tests himself in many ways, most of which have implications for educational and vocational decisions.

The relationship of self-concept and vocational behavior is shown through a series of life stages. During the Growth Stage, which extends up to age 14, the self-concept develops through identification with significant figures in the family and school. Needs and fantasy are dominant early in this stage of vocational development; interest and capacity become more important with increasing social participation and reality-testing. From ages 15 to 24, the Exploration Stage, self-examination, role tryouts, and occupational exploration takes place in school, leisure, and part-time work. In the Establishment Stage, ages 25 to 44, the person has found an appropriate field to implement himself and effort is made to make a permanent place in it. There may be some shifting in finding one's place. Having made a place in the world of work, the Maintenance Stage of 45 to 64 is concerned with holding it. During the Decline Stage, after 65, physical and mental powers decline, work activity changes, and new roles must be developed.

self-concept of disadvantaged children related to behavior

During the formative years a child develops attitudes toward himself and school and toward task performance which profoundly influence his response to academic demands. The typical middle-class child learns to work hard for tangible rewards. The culturally different child learns to take assignments less seriously, because his self-respect depends most on his relations with agemates outside school and little on obtaining approval from adult authority. A child builds an attitude toward school that relates to knowledge and awareness of himself gained from responses of significant others; as they perceive him, so he is influenced to perceive himself.

For example, as the black child is made to feel inadequate and inferior, he rejects his own group and shows hostility toward other groups. The child's unconscious self-hatred results in an indifferent attitude toward school; school is not a pleasant place to be, but a place where he is cunning and mischievious. This is especially the case with black male adolescents, who view the education process as a hostile force tyring to emasculate them. The school, mostly a female enterprise, revolts the male. He rejects all feminine role characteristics and defines school in terms of independence and aggressiveness (Vontress, 1969).

Poussant and Atkinson (1968) explored some of the factors which are relevant in motivating Negro youth. One of the main variables in motivating their behavior is the self-concept. Too frequently the child makes a judgment that he is inferior because he is black. He comes to see himself as an object of scorn and disparagement, unworthy of love and affection, and he learns to reject himself and others like himself. "From that time on, his personality and style of interaction with his environment become modeled and shaped in a warped, self-hating, and self-denigrating way" (p. 242). Of course, Poussant and Atkinson acknowledge that this is a generalization regarding the development of self in black youth to which there are numerous exceptions.

Each of us behaves in accordance with that which is expected. Deutch's (1967) findings indicated that Negro children had significantly more negative self-images than did white children. Like the "self-fulfilling prophecy," blacks were told that they were inferior and would fail, they believed it, and therefore they failed.

Taking a look at the disadvantaged from a different point of view, Greenberg, et al. (1965), found that the poor-achiever, lower-class urban Negro children in fourth grade expressed more positive attitudes than good achievers towards a number of school and authority figure concepts (school, reading, mother). Davidson and Greenberg (1967) found that poor achievers gave significantly higher ratings than the good achievers to school-related concepts. In this study there was also a significant finding for the rating of the self, with the poor achievers assigning more favorable ratings than the good achievers on the potency factor. They attributed the unusual results from these studies to the greater defensive needs of the poor achievers, perhaps especially in the academic area which may be highly anxiety-provoking and threatening to them. It seems that the good achievers were capable of more realistic, and even critical, appraisals. The findings mentioned above were based on the semantic differential instrument. It is interesting to note that, on the Self-Appraisal Scale in the 1967 study, the good achievers were clearly more favorable in their ratings than the poor achievers. It was pointed out that the instrument used was more behaviorally and operationally defined and therefore made the admission of negative self-feelings more tolerable. Consequently, because there is less threat, the poor achiever or the disadvantaged child may be less likely to react with inflated positive ratings.

The studies of Coopersmith (1967) and Rosenberg (1965) found a weak relationship between social class and self-esteem. Coopersmith concluded from his study that apparently the broader social context does not play as important a role in interpreting one's own successes as has often been assumed. Soares and Soares (1970) pointed out the difficulty of generalizing the results of any study because the ability to generalize is limited by the comparability of the populations sampled.

It seems that the disadvantaged child's or minority group member's self-concept is determined by his frame of reference. Previous studies that have found a difference in self-concept between Caucasian and Negro subjects can be recounted as follows. Cases where Negroes were found to hold negative self-concepts would be circumstances where Caucasian individuals or groups were the relevant sources for frames of reference. Conversely, where other Negroes are the reference points, race is not a significant criterion for self-concept appraisal. Unless racial characteristics are an intrinsic part of the situation, role behavior is consistently evaluated by the subject in terms of nonracial role expectations. Findings of the Coleman Report showed overall differences in self-evaluation in school. This could reflect the segregated circumstances under which the Negro subjects were asked to appraise themselves. Other studies where negative Negro self-concepts were found could have been aligned either to the role of "Negro" or to situations where Caucasian frames of reference were used.

Carter (1968) found this to be true in his study of Mexican-American youth. They did not perceive themselves negatively in comparison to their Anglo-Saxon peers. This is because they have their own groups to which they relate, and other social support, and they do not rate themselves in terms of the Anglo society.

The disadvantaged children may have fewer pressures and lower expectation levels placed upon them. However, it is interesting to note that the advantaged middle-class children see themselves in more negative ways. Rosenberg (1965) concluded that the children of old Yankee stock had a lower self-esteem level than that of other groups — perhaps a suprising result, since they tend to possess those status characteristics which are more likely to be associated with high self-esteem. "They are considerably less likely to come from families of low socio-economic status; they are less likely to have poorly educated fathers and mothers; and they are more likely to be taking academic course work (which is positively related to self-esteem). . . And yet this group has a self-esteem level which is actually slightly lower that that of other groups" (pp. 302-303).

From this one can conceive the idea that middle-class children are disadvantaged, perhaps not economically, but psychologically. They go through life trying to prove their self-worth and to build their self-esteem by compensating for their inferiorities.

Halpern (1970) has written a provocative article, "Self Perceptions of Black Children and the Civil Rights Movement." She has given insight concerning the black child's confusion over his parents' identification with or rejection of the civil rights movement, especially the middle-class child whose father has "made it." "For all black children the movement provides a channel through which to express positive or negative feelings for his parents" (p. 520).

relationship between self-concept and drug use. Drugs? Who uses them? Why do they use them? Could it be that those persons who abuse drugs have a negative self-concept and a lower self-esteem? Is it possible that those who experiment with drugs have negative feelings about themselves? The answers to these questions have been sought through research studies by clinicians and other people who work with drug users.

Brehm and Back (1967) investigated the relationship of self-image and attitudes towards drugs. Their study was an attempt to find answers to the question, "Which kind of person would be motivated to change some essential aspect of himself by doing something to his body?" Those typified as users were characterized by feelings of insecurity and willingness to alter the self. Their results gave evidence to two aspects of self perception as leading to a desire for self-modification through physical agents. One is general dissatisfaction with oneself, and the other is the lack of restraints or defenses to use this route to change. The latter includes fear of loss of control, which exists primarily in males, or the defense through denial, which exists primarily in females (the "mental" aspect), and fear of bodily damage. These are conditions which influence the inclination to take drugs and where both factors work consistently in individuals, prediction of inclination to use drugs is quite effective.

It seems that those who use drugs have negative self-perceptions; there is something about themselves that they wish to change and they are willing to use outside agents to facilitate this change, for they are incapable of doing it by themselves.

Schwieder and Kohlon (1969), having interviewing fifty college students in an attempt to find out the reasons for the popularity of LSD, have suggested that most LSD users come from suburban homes. They believe that in this type of living the child is isolated from the imperfect world by his parents. Roles are designated for the individual, and if he conforms and participates in these roles it leads to conformity and tranquility. Consequently this does not allow for reality-testing by the adolescent. Adolescence is a time when it is essential for the young individual to be relatively free to experiment and choose roles. Such an individual plays roles others assign for him, and he never plays his own role of himself.

It is the nature of society that is blamed for the use of LSD, because society today inhibits the development and expression of feeling. Youth wish to feel and experience — to overcome the numbness and tranquility. Even feelings of pain are considered valuable and preferable to having no feeling at all. A majority of students in this study said that with the use of drugs, especially LSD, it is possible for them to relate to others in a meaningful way. Many of the participants expressed the opinion that much was to be gained by the use of a drug which causes one to feel and enables one to talk about one's feelings.

Through the use of drugs the youths feel rapport with humanity, something they were unable to do otherwise, and a new and desired synthesis of intellect and emotion was experienced by those who took LSD and participated in Schwieder and Kohlon's study. This would indicate then, that a motivating factor for taking drugs (especially LSD) was an inability to feel, to experience at an affective level, or to have meaningful relationships with other people.

This would seem to be related to one's own self-concept . To relate to and accept others, we must first accept ourselves. Those who do not accept themselves and have negative self-perceptions or low self-esteem cannot accept others. Others in turn will not accept them. Consequently, they perceive themselves as unacceptable. This is one factor which would account for an inability to relate to other people.

In the suburban isolated type of living, individuals do not have an opportunity to experience and gain a sense of worth. They are busy playing the roles designated for them and not being themselves. This produces the feeling that suburban youth cannot or do not fit in as their own personality would like to dictate. Therefore they have no sense of worth. Without this sense of worth, they possess negative self-perceptions, low self-esteem, and do not accept themselves. They are inhibited, locked in by conformity and tranquility, but dissatisfied with themselves and their experiences. They cannot, by themselves, break away from these patterns. Drugs take away the inhibitions, the negative self-perceptions, the lack of a sense of worth, and enable them to talk about their feelings and to relate to others.

Simon Auster (1969), in his report on "Adolescent Drug Use," made the observation that adolescent drug users seem to fall into several different categories. Drugs are mainly used in the ghetto population to escape from the miserable reality of the users' lives. However, there has been a careful study which has revealed consistent differences between the personalities of addicts and nonaddicts. The addicts have a significant degree of shortsightedness in their judgment; they have a limited capacity for decision-making and purposeful action; they see themselves mainly in negative terms; they are closely tied to their mothers; they are unable to form genuine, close relationships; and they often are badly confused about their sexual feelings. He discusses some of the similarities between users from this group and those from the middle- and upper-class population, in which adolescent users seem to fall into one of three categories.

The first group consists of those who are readily recognized as psychologically disturbed, with or without drugs. This group seems to have more similarity to the lower-class addicts than the other categories. These youngsters' difficulties were prevalent before introduction to drugs; in fact, they show fairly disturbed patterns of family relationships. They are not likely to terminate using drugs until the underlying disturbance begins to be altered. Auster believes that the major element that drugs provide for this group is a "sense of vitality." The ordinary experience of self for these youths is one of an inner void. Here again it is suggested that feeling a sense of being alive is preferred to the void, numbness, and tranquility. Drugs alter internal perceptions and replace the void with some kind of feeling. The second group, and probably the largest, includes those adolescents who will take almost any drug in a social situation because that is what everyone else is doing, because it is the "in" thing to do. These youngsters are using drugs as a way of gaining and reinforcing group acceptance. Auster believes that it is the group pressure that determines the use of drugs and even much of the praise sung about them. He suggests that some in this group have had a therapeutic experience through the use of a hallucinogen, the effect of which was to make the person aware that there is much more to life than his own constricted, limiting perspective had allowed him to see. After using the drug, however, the individual lapsed into a profound depression, the result of realizing how much living he had missed and how much work he would have to do to make up for it.

The second largest group used drugs first out of curiosity and continue to use them intermittently because they find them helpful in clarifying personal questions with which they might be wrestling. The members of this group consistently have adequate and satisfying friendships. However, with their parents they may be cordial and friendly or in a state of armed truce with occasional conflicts. These adolescents on the whole do not come to rely on drugs to face living or cope effectively, but to facilitate them in doing so.

Auster finds the "hippie" group to be a conglomerate rather than a single type. "It contains a large representation of the first, more disturbed, group. Many members of the second group may present themselves as hippie for the same reasons they use drugs; it is the in thing. Occasionally members of the third group go through a personal crisis, often over philosophical issues, that leads to a temporary withdrawal into the hippie community; it has been reported that after about a year or two, they return to their previous state, often with more insight and maturity" (p. 253).

Much of the increase in drug usage among the middle- and upper-class adolescent population lies in the context of contemporary American society much more than in the psychological disturbances of the individual drug users, especially for the third group. In the third group, the use of drugs can be related to a widespread phenomenon of searching for greater self-understanding and significance in living; escaping the alienation, confusion, and uncertainty so rampant in contemporary society; and a wish to become able to grasp the presence of the moment and live their lives, fully and with immediacy.

Because the contemporary world has undergone such "massive structural change" and the advances in technology have changed our style of living and the structure of our environment, people can no longer rely on the reference standards applied in earlier years to assess situations which causes confusion and uncertainty. Consequently, there has been a quest for self-awareness and understanding, anything which would intensify internal experience so as to bring into awareness heretofore unrecognized responses that may help in making an assessment of a complex and puzzling situation. Therefore, some have turned to drugs through which internal perceptions of sensation, thought, and feeling are heightened. People have also turned to other avenues for their self-discovery potential, such as group experiences and Eastern forms of meditation.

The problem with the youngsters who rely exclusively on drugs is that they have so little sense of self. They have a sense of futility about life and relationships which leads them to mistrust all relationships, including those with their peers, and to turn inward for answers and relief.

One cannot help asking why so many young people experience so little self-worth. As we have seen so far, it is because of our contemporary society and poor family relationships. In an article on drug use in school-age children, Randall (1970) hints at some other answers. He makes the observation that children who have problems in learning, are disruptive in class, and show evidence of neglect or rejection, are frequently among those youngsters who experiment with drugs. Rejection, inappropriate behavior, punishment, negative self-concept, and low self-esteem seem to be elements involved in drug usage. Children begin to use drugs in the upper elementary grades, and their number increases significantly at the junior high age. Glue sniffers have been described as having low self-esteem, being anxious and passive, and having poor personality adjustment. Other studies have shown that students apprehended as "sniffers" have had a history of delinquency prior to practicing this abuse. Their past history indicates poor school adjustment, low achievement, and unsatisfactory home life.

Dearden (1971) has concluded from his findings that drug use among students is a social phenomenon. The use of drugs, except heroin, usually occurs in groups. They have a high need for recognition and acceptance and they gain attention in small groups through verbal activity and occasional aggressiveness. Through drugs the group shared a common experience which brings about cohesiveness among members. Drug users support each other, providing an atmosphere in which each can feel secure, cared about, and important as a human being. He suggests that, until the school meets the personal needs of students, they will be drawn into the drug group for recognition, acceptance, identity, self-esteem, and leadership. It has been shown that if students are made to feel accepted and respected by peers, teachers, and parents, there is a reduction in the use of drugs or a discontinuance of their use. But, as it stands, students tend to be dissatisfied with teachers and believe most are insensitive and unconcerned with them as human beings.

Jacobson (1970) presents views on drug abuse and learning effects. She brings into focus one of the main problems which contributes to young people's turning to drugs — that is, the educational institutions' lack of emphasis, even willingness to ignore, the humanistic approach, which teaches the philosophy of human dignity, personal worth, self-knowledge, and individual understanding. The young people's world is surrounded with feelings of anxiety, self-consciousness, ambivalence towards parents, fear, distrust, loneliness, and rebellion. A confusing factor to many adults is that the young are at times very sophisticated but not necessarily mature. They find it difficult to establish relationships, not just between parent and children, but between "people and people." Through their use of drugs, tensions, problems, and anxieties may be lessened, resulting in the lack of necessity and frequently the inability to experience the decisions and strains associated with the natural stages of growth and development. The young drug user thereby forfeits many opportunities to learn to cope with problems and to develop capacities needed for advancement toward a greater maturity.

Hill (1968), writing about marijuana and alcohol in the youth culture, advocates that integrity crisis is fast replacing the identity crisis with young people, especially as they attempt to meet the challenges of the megalopolis, which represents a fast-changing society and an accelerating technology. Where identity crisis refers to a state of testing, experimenting, and rebelling, lasting various lengths of time, wherein one has the implicit aim of eventually being able to accept and affirm adult authority together with the prevailing values, roles, and institutions, the integrity crisis "refers to a state of experimentation and rebellion which involves a suspension of behavior directed towards assuming and/or trying

out conventional psychological identities" (p. 291). It is characterized by a directionless state of being — or "hanging loose." An
individual in a state of identity suspension is likely to possess certain attitudes and values toward our present society which tend to
lead him temporarily to "drop out" in various ways and to varying
degrees, both intentionally and unintentionally, from conventional
ways of perceiving and behaving. There are various ways of dropping out, including by "turning on" with marijuana, which represent some sort of conscious or unconscious attempts at psychological renewal.

Hill suggests that in order to find one's self an individual must
exert enormously more initiative, originality, and reflectiveness in
addition to discovering his *own* authority. Perhaps a change in
perspective or an alteration of consciousness may be what is
needed to live in this new era effectively. This does not necessarily have to be accomplished by drugs, for there are many other
more convenient, less hazardous, and more significant ways to
achieve a state of changed consciousness simply through "broad-
ening the spectrum of one's relationships."

Throughout all of the research and literature there seem to be
ideas or thoughts reiterated. In summary, some of these are that
those who use drugs generally have negative self-concepts, low
self-esteem, and poor body images. They are incapable of having
meaningful relationships without the use of drugs. There is a general search for self-understanding and a desire to experience,
whether it be pleasure or pain, to feel, to be able to give expression to those feelings. Drugs are used to increase perception, to
aid in shaking loose old and restricted perceptions. The society at
large is responsible for the use of drugs. The society inhibits the
development and expression of feeling and, because of vast
changes in the world, reference points are no longer adequate.
Adolescents need to reality-test and to experiment with various
roles. Society that is conforming does not allow for this and the
use of drugs seems to erase the potential for doing so.

conclusion

The importance of one's self-concept to his behavior pattern is
evident in the areas presented. Only a few areas of self-concept
and behavior have been explored in this chapter, however they
can serve to illustrate the relationship of self-concept to behavior.

The reader will be able to apply the conceptualization in understanding many other behaviors.

From the areas examined here, the importance of the social learning of one's self-concept becomes apparent. The child gains a concept of himself through interacting with others. In striving to be consistent with that concept, he behaves in ways that are rewarded or punished by significant people, which affects the concept he has of himself, which in turn contributes to a behavior pattern — and so the circle goes. Now we must explore ways of intervention which can be used to enhance the self-concept of youth.

references

Auster, S. L. "Adolescent Drug Use." *Educational Leadership* 27 (1968): 281-86.

Brehm, M., and Back, K. "Self-Image and Attitudes toward Drugs." *Journal of Personality* 36 (1967): 299-313.

Borislaw, B. "Self-Evaluation and Academic Achievement." *Journal of Counseling Psychology* 9 (1962): 246-54.

Brookover, W. B., *et al.*, *Self-Concept of Ability and School Achievement, II* (Second report on the Continuing Study of Relationships of Self-Concept and Achievement. Final Report on Cooperative Research Project, Improving Academic Achievement Through Student's Self-Concept Enhancement), Michigan State University College of Education, Bureau of Education Research Service, October 1965.

Carter, T. P. "The Negative Self-Concept of Mexican-American Students." *School and Society* 96 (1968): 217-19.

Campbell, P. B. "Self-Concept and Academic Achievement in Middle Grade Public School Children." *Dissertation Abstracts* 27 (1966): 1535-36.

Combs, A. W. "Intelligence from a Perceptual Point of View." *Journal of Abnormal and Social Psychology* 49 (1952): 562-73.

Coopersmith, S. *The Antecedents of Self-Esteem.* San Francisco: W. H. Freemen and Co., Publishers, 1967.

Davidson, H., and Greenberg, J. *School Achievers from a Deprived Background.* New York: Associated Educational Services Corporation, 1967.

Dearden, M. H. "Observations about Student Use of Drugs." *School Management* 15 (May 1971): 10.

Fink, M. B. "Self-Concept as it Relates to Academic Achievement." In *The Self in Growth Teaching and Learning,* edited by D. Hamachek. Englewood Cliffs, N. J.: Prentice-Hall, Inc., 1965.

Fromm-Reichmann, F. "Psychiatric Aspects of Anxiety." In *Identity and Anxiety,* edited by M. Stein, A. J. Uedich, and D. M. White. Glencoe, Ill.: The Free Press, 1960.

Greenberg, J.; Grever, J. M.; Chall, J.; Davidson, H. H. "Attitudes of Children from a Deprived Environment toward Achievement Related Concepts." *Journal of Educational Research* 59 (1965): 57-62.

Halpern, F. "Self-Perception of Black Children and the Civil Rights Movement." *American Journal of Orthopsychiatry* 40 (1970): 520-26.

Hamachek, D. E. *Encounters with the Self.* New York: Holt, Rinehart & Winston, Inc., 1971.

Hill, W. T. "The 'High' and 'Low' of Marijuana and Alcohol in the Youth Culture." *Soundings* 51 (Fall 1968) 290-307.

Hogan, E. O., and Green, R. L. "Can Teachers Modify Children's Self-Concepts?" *Teachers College Record* 72 (1971): 423-26.

Horney, K. *Neurosis and Human Growth.* New York: W. W. Norton & Company, Inc., 1950.

Kaplon, B. L. "Anxiety: A Classroom Close-Up." *The Elementary School Journal* 71 (November 1970): 70-77.

La Benne, W. D., and Greene, B. I. *Educational Implications of Self-Concept Theory.* Pacific Palisades, Cal.: Goodyear Publishing Company, Inc., 1969.

Lecky, P. *Self-Consistency: A Theory of Personality.* New York: Island Press, 1945.

Osipow, S. *Theories of Career Development.* New York: Appleton-Century-Crofts, 1968.

Poussant, A. F., and Atkinson, C. "Negro Youth and Psychological Motivation." *Journal of Negro Education* 37 (1968): 241-51.

Purkey, W. W. *Self-Concept and School Achievement.* Englewood Cliffs, N. J.: Prentice-Hall, Inc., 1970.

Rosenberg, M. *Society and the Adolescent Self-Concept.* Princeton, N. J.: Princeton University Press, 1965.

Schwieder, R. M., and Kohlon, R. "The Tranquil Society — Or Why LSD." *The Record* 70 (April 1969): 627-33.

Shaw, M. C.; Edson, K.; Bell, H. "The Self-Concept of Bright Under-achieving High School Students as Revealed by Adjective Check List." *The Personnel and Guidance Journal* 39 (1960): 193.

Shaw, M. C., McCuen, J. T. "The Onset of Academic Underachievement in Bright Children." *Journal of Educational Psychology* 51 (1960): 103-108.

Snygg, D., and Combs, A. W. *Individual Behavior.* New York: Harper and Brothers, 1949.

Strong, O. J., and Feder, D. D. "Measurement of the Self-Concept." *Journal of Counseling Psychology* 8 (1961): 170-78.

Super, D. E. "Vocational Adjustment: Implementing a Self-Concept." *Occupations* 30 (1951): 88-92.

Vontress, C. E. "The Modern Counselor and the Culturally Different." *Education* 89 (April 1969): 359-63.

Wattenberg, W. W., and Clifford, C. "Relation of Self-Concept to Beginning Achievement in Reading." *Child Development* 35 (1964): 461-67.

Wylie, R. *Self-Concept: A Critical Survey of the Pertinent Research Literature.* Lincoln: University of Nebraska Press, 1961.

four * the counselor and
self-concept

Many youths are searching for meaning, which is primarily a
search for self. So many people seem to be burdened with negative or only semi-positive self-concepts and so few to be blessed
with healthy, positive self-concepts. We must question seriously
why this seems so. What is it in our world, our society, our institutions, and our interpersonal relationships that puts and keeps so
many people on the negative side of the ledger? These are significant concerns, since the self-concept of the individuals are the
pivotal determinants of their perception of the outside world and
thus their behavior in that world.

That counselors and other human relations workers are asked
to deal with the construct herein called self-concept is not the
question. Rather, this final chapter will attempt to deal with some
possible techniques or procedures for enhancing self-concept.
Counselors have long been involved in the self-concept as a significant factor in the counseling process and as an important vari-
able in the evaluation of counseling. Wrenn (1958) adhered very
closely to the notions, then in vogue, of the counselor's dealing
with self-concepts almost exclusively through psychological counseling. The counselor was foremost a psychologist and dealt with

faulty or negative self-concept as adjustive inner-based problems. There is still a need for counselors to deal with some conceptions of self in this manner. Therefore certain techniques of long proven worth and traditional base must be called forth. Such techniques as individual and group counseling are presented; however, we have proposed them as a process of moving from self-exploration to self-understanding to change in behavior. This active participation of the counselor in changing self-concept and behavior is frequently different from helping a student to gain insight and then assuming the change in behavior will occur. If a student is able to think differently about himself and modify his behavior, the environment must be conducive to these changes. Lasting change in the student cannot be incurred without changing the social situation. The last section in this chapter discusses consulting with significant adults and working with school environment to produce a more conducive situation for positive self-development.

individual counseling

Changing a student's self-concept in individual counseling is not easy. Even when he is not satisfied with himself, changing feelings or behaviors will be threatening. The defense system is ready to ward off encounters. Of all the tasks outlined as part of the counselor's role, counseling is probably one of the most difficult to perform. The counselor needs to provide a relationship that is safe enough for the student to drop some of the defenses and explore himself. As a student explores, he can develop new insights and understanding of himself which can lead to behavior changes. The counselor can be an active participant in the process, stimulating the explorations, insights, and understanding, and assisting in the changing of behaviors. Some of the behavior changes may be covert and deal with new feelings or attitudes toward himself. In many cases, these should lead to overt behavior changes. Success in the overt behaviors will also reinforce a more positive self-concept.

There is a theoretical basis for this concept of counseling. Recall that in the development of personality every individual is the center of his own world. The individual reacts to his phenomenal field as he experiences and perceives it, and his perceptions are his reality. As a result of his interactions with the environment, and particularly as a result of interactions with others, a structure of self is formed. As experiences occur, the individual can symbolize them and include them into some relationship to the self; ignore them because he doesn't perceive their relationship to the self structure; or deny them symbolization or distort their symbolization because they are inconsistent with his self structure. Psychological adjustment occurs when the concept of the self includes all the sensory and visual experiences of the person on a symbolic level with his self-concept. Psychological maladjustment exists when a person denies significant experiences which are therefore not symbolized or organized into his self structure. Under conditions involving absence of threat to the self structure, experiences which are inconsistent with it may be examined and the self-concept revised to include such experiences. The assumption is, then, that the person will have new feelings or attitudes about himself which will lead to behavior modification.

establishing a relationship

The first major concern of the counselor is to provide the situation which reduces the threat to self-concept and thereby permits the student to explore himself. Rogers (1957) stated what he called the necessary and sufficient conditions for personality change. These are specific counselor attitudes which are believed to be essential for the development of a counseling relationship. If the counselor is to be helpful with the student, a relationship must exist. This means the two individuals must be in psychological contact, have an awareness of each other, and work together. The other necessary conditions postulated by Rogers include the counselor's being genuine in the relationship, experiencing positive regard for the client, and expressing empathic understanding.

The counselor must be genuine or congruent in the relationship. The counselor must not be a facade or a role or a pretense, but must behave exactly as he feels. He not only means what he says, but his feeling also matches what he is expressing. To be congruent, the counselor must be willing to be and to express the words, behavior, feelings, and attitudes that exist within him. This is the only way the relationship can have reality for the client.

Another facilitative condition in the relationship is the counselor's experiencing an empathic understanding of the client's world and being able to communicate this to the client. The counselor senses the feelings and personal meanings which the client is experiencing. When he is able to perceive these as they seem to the client and can successfully communicate some of this understanding to the client, this condition is fulfilled.

Another condition of a safe counseling relationship is the counselor's experiencing a warm, positive, accepting attitude toward the client. Although this is listed third, it probably is the first thing which the counselor is able to communicate to the client. It means that he likes the client as a person and cares for him in a non-possessive way as a person with potentiality. The counselor respects the client as a separate individual and gives him positive regard. The more the positive regard is unconditional, the more effective and safer the relationship will be. The fewer the conditions a counselor places on the client the more unconditional his positive regard will be. This means that there are no conditions or strings attached. It is a type of acceptance of and regard for the person's attributes at the moment no matter how negative or positive they may be. This acceptance of the fluctuating feelings of the client makes a relationship warm and safe. It means the client does not have to hide parts of himself, behave in certain ways, or play a certain game for the counselor to pay attention to him, or to like him as a person.

Rogers has contributed the most focus on these variables and their importance in the relationship. In fact, the concept of the necessary and sufficient conditions for change are frequently viewed as synonymous with client-centered counseling or a self theory approach to counseling. However, most approaches to the counseling relationship include similar variables. Learning theory approaches to counseling, suggested by Dollard and Miller (1950), discuss similar variables for the counseling relationship. Even the most action-oriented counselors who use conditioning approaches in counseling describe relationship variables which are quite similar to those of other approaches to counseling. Wolpe (1966) states that whatever else the counselor may do, it is of first importance to display empathy and establish a trustful relationship. The client must feel fully accepted as a human being and not less worthy or less fortunate than the counselor. He believes that the specific techniques used in counseling must be administered by persons who are able to treat the client with respectful seriousness and who can communicate a sincere desire to be of service.

Carkhuff and Berenson (1967) have used the concept of these conditions to establish an eclectic approach to counseling. They refined, extended, and researched these concepts to the point of establishing a model for counseling. They described this as a comprehensive model of facilitative processes. They employ the same conditions of empathy, respect, and genuineness, and include a new condition called concreteness.

To make these conditions less abstract and more measureable, Carkhuff (1967) developed a five-point scale to access the level of the facilitative dimensions. This permits the operationalization of the dimensions and relates improved functioning of the client to higher offered conditions by the counselor. On all scales, level three is defined as minimally facilitative interpersonal functioning. At level three, the counselor's response of empathic understanding is essentially interchangeable with those of the client in that they express essentially the same affect and meaning. The positive respect and understanding for the client's feelings, experiences, and potentials are communicated, and the counselor provides no discrepancies between what he verbally states and the other cues indicative of his feeling. The counselor's response to the relevant concreteness of the client is defined as the counselor's enabling the client to discuss personally relevant material in a specific and concrete terminology.

Below level three, the responses of the counselor detract from those of the client. At level two, the counselor does respond to the expressed feeling of the client, but he does so in such a way that he subtracts noticeably from the affective communication of the client, and the counselor's response to the client is made in such a way that he communicates little respect or concern for the feelings and experiences of the client. There are also indications that the counselor's responses are slightly interrelated to what other cues indicate he is feeling at the moment. The counselor frequently leads or allows the discussion of material which is relevant to the client to be dealt with on a somewhat vague or abstract level. At the first level, there is communication of a clear lack of respect or negative regard for the client and the counselor's expressions are clearly unrelated to other cues which indicate his feelings at the moment, and his general responses are negative in regard to the client's. At the first level, the counselor's responses do not attend or distract significantly from the expression of the client in such a way that he does not understand the client; in fact, he leads or allows the discussion with the client to deal only with vague and anonymous generalizations.

Above level three, the counselor's responses are additive in nature, so that at level four the responses of the counselor add noticeably to the expression of the client in such a way as to express feelings of a deeper level than the client is expressing himself.

The counselor's communications create a deep respect for the client and he presents positive cues indicating a human response, whether it is positive or negative, in a nondestructive manner to the client. The counselor is frequently helpful in enabling the client to develop more fully in concrete and specific words his emphasis of concern. At the fifth level, the counselor's responses add significantly to the feelings and meaning of the client in such a way as to express accurate feelings beyond what the person is able to express. He communicates a very deep respect for the client's worth as a person and his potential as a free individual, and his expressions indicate that he is freely and deeply himself in his relationship with the client. He is completely spontaneous in his action and open to all of his experiences. The counselor's communications are always helpful in getting discussion, so that the client may discuss fluently, directly, and completely specific feelings and experiences.

the counseling process

The process of counseling would involve the counselor's providing a facilitative relationship in which the client would feel safe enough to explore himself and his life's situation. This self-exploration would lead to a greater degree of self-understanding as well as a better understanding of his environment. Ideally this increased understanding would lead to the person's changing behavior to be more effective. When the person is able to behave more effectively, he will feel better about himself and therefore have an increase in self-regard. In many cases, however, the understanding does not lead directly to change in behavior and the counselor must intervene to help the student try some new behaviors.

Several studies have demonstrated that differential effects of counselor-offered facilitative conditions affect the self-exploration of high and low functioning clients (Holder, et al., 1967; Piaget, et al., 1967). For the higher functioning client, the variance in the counselor-offered conditions has little effect on his level of self-exploration. Such a client appears to have enough confidence in himself that he explores himself even when the counselor is not highly facilitative. However, the lower functioning client, or the client with a poorer self-concept, is affected considerably by the different levels of counselor-offered conditions; that is, he is able to explore himself much more fully when the therapist offers higher levels of facilitation.

self-exploration. Carkhuff has proposed a five-point scale to examine self-exploration. At the first level the client avoids any self-description or self-exploration which would reveal personal feelings to the counselor. At this level the client probably does not trust his own feelings and may not like himself well enough to offer his inner feelings to the counselor. This lack of self-exploration is a common occurance in beginning counseling. At the second level of self-exploration the client will respond with discussion to the introduction of personally relevant material by the counselor. His response, however, is mechanical in manner and does not demonstrate any real feeling. The client is answering questions about himself, giving conclusions he has already reached about his self-concept, but not exploring himself. At this level the counselor will be able to learn much about the client's present self-concept. At the third level the client voluntarily introduces discussions of personally relevant material but does so mechanically and without demonstrating much feeling. This frequently is a volunteering of material that he has already rehearsed with himself or possibly has discussed with other persons previously. There is no spontaneity and no inward probing for new feelings or experiences. At the fourth level the client voluntarily introduces personally relevant material in a spontaneous manner. The client is dealing with his present feeling level. This behavior may lead to the fifth level in which the client actively and spontaneously probes into newly discovered feelings and experiences about himself and his situation.

What are some things the counselor can do to help the client in his self-exploration? As well as presenting the various levels to conceptualize the client's self-exploration, Carkhuff (1971) has also suggested a number of guidelines to assist the counselor in the exploratory stage of counseling. First, the counselor must establish client exploration as his immediate goal. Without this starting point the client will not gain new insights, gain new understanding, or be able to incorporate new behaviors into his pattern. Second, the counselor needs initially to understand the client at the level of self-exploration he presents. Exploration of personal material is most likely to occur when there is an understanding and suspension of attitude or judgment by the counselor. The client will move increasingly toward initiating his exploration and toward spontaneity of his emotions if the counselor is willing to accept him at each level. Third, the counselor should initially offer minimal facilitative levels of the facilitative conditions.

When the counselor offers minimal levels of empathy, respect, concreteness, and genuineness he establishes a relationship which the client can explore himself, experiment and experience himself. The minimal facilitative conditions enable the client to know that the counselor understands him on his terms and also provides him with the feedback necessary for later reformulations. Fourth, the counselor should employ the client's self-sustaining level of self-exploration as a guide for moving to the next stage in the counseling process. Within a given problem or topic area, the criterion for movement to the next stage of counseling can be the client's ability to deal with his own explorations. When the client is able to do this, the counselor can proceed in focusing upon the client's self-understanding or action, depending on the client's understanding. Fifth, the counselor should recognize a repetition of the cycle of self-exploration both within and between different content areas. When the client works through the process and is able to explore himself in terms of a situation with his parents, for example, he may begin at the first level of self-exploration when the topic turns to his relationship with his peers or a teacher.

self-understanding. When the client is able to deal with his own exploration and the immediate feelings, the counselor can help draw together the fragmented insights and help the client develop self-understanding. The counselor can focus on the construction or reconstruction of the client's communication process. More effective intrapersonal, as well as interpersonal, communication is a primary goal leading to constructive action. The counselor may begin by focusing on the client's more competent areas. In other words, the probability of the client's understanding and acting upon his situation is greatest in the areas in which he is functioning at the highest levels. Success in these experiences will increase the probability of understanding and action in other areas. The counselor may offer minimal levels of facilitative conditions as he establishes the relationship and the client begins to explore himself. With greater exploration and an improvement in self-understanding, the counselor can increase his level of facilitative conditions. This is exemplified when the client is safe enough to explore himself and is gaining new insight; he is able to handle additive responses within the given content areas. As the client gains in self-understanding and is able to sustain his level of effective understanding, the counselor can focus attention on the next stage of counseling: action. He needs to recognize a repetition in the cycle of self-exploration to understanding to action. The early phase of self-exploration and understanding may lead to some action. This action will provide feedback which can modify the original concepts and elicit further explorations leading to a deeper level of understanding, and culminating in new action.

action. The ultimate goal for the counselor should be to help the client toward constructive action. The ultimate goal of counseling is constructive action for the client, both in terms of himself and his situation. There is an interrelatedness between the client's self-understanding and his action, with each serving to sharpen the other. The counselor emphasizes action in the area in which the client best understands himself. This offers the highest probability of successful action. As the client increases in other areas of understanding and approaches action, the counselor can increase his level of action orientation. Carkhuff (1971) suggests that the counselor begins to initiate more activities based on his experience in the situation, thus serving as both a model and agent for the client to do likewise. Again the increase in action is employed to increase higher levels of understanding and therefore more constructive action in the problem areas. While the emphasis is on acting according to one's experience, the counselor attempts to insure generalization of learning and acting in relationships outside the counseling situation. This can be done more effectively when a full description of the goals of counseling can be achieved. When the counselor and client are able to describe the dimensions desired, a plan can be put into operation to meet those goals. Vague goals are not helpful in developing procedures for attainment. When operational goals have been established, step-by-step procedures for their attainment can be developed. Each step represents a systematic progression toward the goal. The more fully the goals have been described, the more fully the steps can be described and implemented. Once the client is able to employ constructive action in one area, the counselor can repeat the cycle in another problem area; that is, once the client has been able to put into action some new behaviors this will have an effect on his self-concept and he will have more confidence in attempting new action. When the client demonstrates increasing ability to act constructively in all the relevant problem areas (goals), he is indicating a readiness for termination.

group experiences

Much of what we believe about ourselves comes from the feedback we have gathered from our interactions with other people. Group experiences provide the opportunity for each person to give and receive direct feedback on his behaviors. Direct feedback is important because, as we interact with others, we must draw conclusions about what these interactions mean. Normal everyday interactions do not allow us to check the reactions of others — as can be done in a group experience. If everyone offers a piece of feedback, the receiver has the right to demand clarification and justification of this feedback. By asking for specific behavioral indications of feedback within certain limits the group allows its members to deal with the here and now. By being forced to analyze his behavior in the group, here and now, one can see how he acts in the everyday world. The group is only a microcosm of society, and while people try hard to mask certain behaviors, the same self one displays in the real world will emerge. The group can help a person examine and understand his self-concept and hence help him interpret his behaviors.

What is a group? A group is more than a collection of people. They share some common attitudes and values, accept each other, and relate to each other in many ways. They desire membership in the group to deal with problems they have in common as well as to satisfy some individual problems. They desire this membership enough to conform at least minimally to the group standards. Cartwright and Zander (1968) offer the following statements as characteristic of individuals in groups:

> They engage in frequent interactions;
> They define themselves as group members;
> They are defined by others as belonging to the group;
> They share norms concerning matters of common interest;
> They participate in a system of interlocking roles;
> They identify with one another as a result of having set up the same model — objective — or ideals in their superego;
> They find the group to be rewarding;
> They pursue promotively interdependent goals;
> They have a collective perception of their unity;
> They tend to act in a unitary manner toward the environment (p. 48).

The more of these characteristics the group members have, the stronger the group will be. One can see that from this kind of meaningful interaction with other people a person would be able to receive meaningful feedback and learn about himself.

Loser (1957) discussed the essential properties of a group as: dynamic interaction, having a common goal, and appropriate number of members for the proposed function, their volition and consent, and developing a capacity for self-direction. It is necessary for some type of relationship, and subsequent interaction based on this relationship, to develop if the members are going to learn from each other. The kind of feedback they want and the willingness to give to each other will depend upon having a common goal. For students wanting to examine themselves and secure feedback for developing a self-concept, a rather small number of members are necessary. The concept of volition and consent for counseling in schools is particularly important. An effective group functions only in terms of the volition and consent of its members, and the students who are involuntary members will not explore themselves in a group and will not be open to feedback regarding themselves. If the group is voluntary and becomes meaningful there will be a willingness to govern and control themselves and the group will move in terms of self-direction.

There are several levels and degrees of group work that are appropriate. Group guidance consists of task oriented situations which are usually short-term (one to ten sessions) with rather large groups (up to a class size of approximately 25). These sessions can be useful in dispensing and discussing information and permitting a student to see that many other students have the same needs for information and experience some of the same difficulties and perceptions of themselves or a situation.

Another level of group activity may be called an affective discussion group. Such a group would have a smaller number of students who would be able to discuss problems and project themselves into problem situations which would permit them to examine how they would feel in similar circumstances. This is somewhat like taking a fantasy trip.

A third level of group activity involves group counseling. These groups are small, usually six to twelve people, and interaction is encouraged between group members. The group members are usually brought together because they have a common problem or they are a relatively compatible group of adolescents who can help each other with developmental problems which move along a continuum from specific to general.

It is important to understand some differences in the roles of content and process within the group. There is more emphasis on leader control and a focus on facts in a group guidance situation which moves to a less content-oriented meeting with more feelings, attitudes and values expressed in a discussion group. In a discussion group the topic may be introduced by the leader, and he will participate, but everyone has a chance to talk. In group counseling the content really involves the participants as individuals. There is not an external content but they do talk about themselves. There is a great deal of emphasis on feelings, attitudes and values and there is a process involving interaction with less control from the leader.

group guidance

Group guidance is frequently used for the dissemination of information. It may be argued that large groups are more correctly termed collections of individuals rather than groups. It is important for the counselor to attempt to create at least some aspects of the group within such a collection of individuals in order to facilitate a student's learning. It is important that the group topic mean something to the students, therefore they share some common goal in being there. If the group is to have an effect on one another there must be some interaction between them.

Group guidance activities can be effective in transmitting information that affects the student's self-concept and behavior. Large groups can be used to interpret test results. From a good test interpretation, a student may learn something about his abilities, aptitudes, or interests that could affect the way he thinks about himself. Armed with such data, he should be able to make more appropriate educational and vocational decisions. In a similar way educational and vocational information can be communicated in large groups which help students understand themselves in terms of opportunities. Varenhorst and Gelatt (1971) propose group guidance as an effective tool to teach students decision-making. This process involves the students' awareness of themselves as well as external forces.

Counselors must cope with two major concerns in dealing with large-group guidance. First, there is a tendency for the students to be just passive listeners, therefore one cannot be certain if they understand the information. Second, if the information is being received, is it being received accurately and what does it mean personally to the student?

Large-group guidance activities will be organized by the counselor and it is he who probably determines the goal of the group. He must have in mind what he expects for them to accomplish and must plan for the achievement of this goal. It is important that the information he is going to communicate be accurate, relevant to the students, and something that they can apply. The information must be important to the students and there should be some discussion as to how they can use it. If they are unable to use the data or work out steps to use it, the information is worthless. It is also important to deal with the feedback from the students. The counselor must present the information so that the student can use the facts with a minimum of transfer. The activity needs to be presented in such a way that it will stimulate the interest. A counselor may use drawings, slides, film, handouts, or other types of audio-visual aids. A panel may discuss a topic before a group. A symposium may include short talks by individuals. Either of these could include a forum in which the audience is given an opprotunity to participate.

The second problem — does the student understand the information that was provided? — necessitates the counselor's receiving some type of feedback, or organizing the situation so that the students are able to get feedback from each other. This may be done by the use of buzz sessions in which the larger group is broken up into smaller groups to discuss a specific aspect that was presented. Delegates from each small group then can report back to the large group. Another alternative, of course, is to use smaller-sized groups, which would permit the students and the counselor to discuss and interact about the content of the group.

discussion groups

Cramer and Herr (1971) define the term *affective discussion* as "...a type of activity which bridges the gap between purely intellective emphases within a tight structure — the sterotype of group guidance — and gut level responses emphasized in group counseling." The role of the discussion leader would be more active than one in a counseling group, but less structured than in a large-group guidance situation. The student will probably not reveal as much "self" in an affective discussion as he would in group counseling, but the student may think about himself as much. The affective discussion aims at projection, so that the student puts himself in the place of another and feels how he would feel in that situation. It provides for a reality testing condition for the student and gives him the latitude within a structured setting to test his perceptions of self against environmental possibilities or probabilities. Such discussion groups are largely developmental and preventive. The groups do not need to meet on any protracted basis as counseling groups generally do, but may meet as topics arise. For example, students who are considering a choice of college may discuss the feelings that they have about going away to school vs. staying at home. Through the affective discussion a student can project himself into the situation and feel how it would be to live away from home at a large university. He can feel, and maybe discuss, the concerns he has, and thereby have some reality testing of what the feelings would be and how he might behave in that situation. In most cases discussion groups do not meet the criteria for being a group, however students can gain feedback from each other and learn about themselves as they project themselves into the topic.

group counseling

The purpose of group counseling is to assist the individuals to a fuller realization and acceptance of themselves and others. Group counseling provides the student with an opportunity to redefine certain perceptions of himself as he interacts with other individuals. The group is more powerful than the counselor and this power can be exercised in two directions. Because the group is made up of peer members, the feedback from the peers regarding the self is more potent and more important to the student than that of a single counselor. The group feedback can give consensus regarding their perceptions of the individual's behavior. Consensus from the group will be more powerful than the person's self-insight or the feedback from the counselor. However, the group can exert power against the counselor in an attempt to protect the individual. That is, the individual will feel more secure in a group of peers that he would in meeting the counselor in a one-to-one relationship. Therefore the group can provide an element of security. Obviously the individuals will meet more of the criteria Loser, Cartwright, and Zander describe as essential to being considered a group.

The group also provides an opportunity for the individual to have reality testing. The group is a microcosm of society and as the individual gains feedback—has a new self-understanding—he is able to try out new behaviors in this group setting, receiving additional feedback which can be used to test the reality of his self-concept and his new behaviors. By working many of these out in the group prior to testing them in the larger society, the student will have more confidence.

Kelman (1963) suggested three types of behavior that are needed to be induced within the counseling situation for behavior modification to occur: compliance, identification, and internalization. Each of these behaviors is associated with a particular stage in the counseling process: compliance with engaging in the counseling process; identification with commitment to the purposes of the group; and internalization with the occurance of behavior-modifying experiences. Through this process the student will experience the same progression as in individual counseling: self-exploration leading to self-understanding leading to behavior change.

engagement in the process. In order for the group to move forward effectively and for the student to learn about himself and eventually change behaviors, he must become involved in the process. Most individuals approaching a group have ambivalent feelings about it. They would like to improve their behavior but they are frightened about the experience and in most cases do not really want to change. It is important for the counselor to help the student deal with these ambivalent feelings by communicating that it is common and appropriate to have them and that these resistances are things that can be talked about. In some ways the counselor is a model for behaviors during this period of time. He will probably direct the tone of the meeting by following some things and ignoring others. If he is an active counselor he may interpret statements and on occasions may confront a student. If he is more non-directive he will show the direction he wishes to go by responding to some statements and not to others. The student responds to such cues and learns to act appropriately; that is, he is learning to play the game by the counselor's rules. The danger, of course, is that the student is doing just that — playing the game. A student could learn the right phrases without any emotional involvement. If he is just at a superficial level he will not really have a meaningful insight that will lead to behavioral change. Although the counselor is important in the process of counseling, other members will also sanction behaviors and put pressure on others to conform to the group standards. One of the strongest pressures is the individual's desire to become accepted by the other group members. During the engagement stage, the counselor and the group members cooperate in creating a situation in which each student becomes engaged in the process of counseling. Once this has occurred, the student has to decide how much of a commitment to counseling he is willing to make.

commitment to the process. The student must be personally committed to the counseling process for real behavioral change to occur. A student must be motivated to stay with the group for him to benefit from it. He needs to be free to express himself, to explore himself with the group. If he does not perceive the group situation as a safe one, his defense mechanisms will remain intact and he will not explore himself. Without the exploration he will not deal with the feedback from the other members of the group and will not gain new self-understanding. Identification with the group is essential to the building of meaningful relationships between the group members. The student learns that he is accepted for what he is, even including his obvious deficiencies. This acceptance may be more important to the individual than being accepted by the counselor. The individual's commitment to the process of counseling will also be fostered by his membership in the group. He will discover that he is not isolated and that there are other people with similar difficulties. This awareness of similar difficulties and a common fate increases the individual's identification with the group and his personal commitment to it. There is a danger, however, that an individual may come to feel so completely accepted by the group that, although he has additional feedback about himself, it does not lead to behavioral change. It is important for individuals to be accepted, but they must move beyond the point of dependence on the group.

behavior change. In the first stage of the group, the student may just be playing a game. In the second stage, changes are dependent upon the relationships of the group members, and on his internalization of a new, more realistic, behavior pattern. This is brought about by the student's objective evaluation of his past behavior; through his self-exploration and with feedback from the group members he is able to examine his feelings and behaviors and recognize their distorted and frequently self-defeating aspects. As a result of new insight and understanding, he may develop a more realistic attitude and behavior pattern. Reality testing within the group continues to give the student behavior-modifying experiences. When he exhibits his old behavior patterns, he can be confronted not only with their self-defeating nature but also with the reaction which that behavior elicits in other people. He can build on the experience in the group and apply this learning to other situations in his daily life.

consultation

significant adults

The behavior of the child is related to his self-concept, which is determined by the interaction he has with other significant individuals. Therefore it is important that the student's adaptive behavior be reinforced in his environment. It is paramount that guidance extend beyond the counseling session to promote changes in behavior and self-understanding. The counselor may need to alert teachers and parents to the significance of certain adaptive and maladaptive behaviors that occur in their relationships with the student and to enlist their help in changing the self-concept and behavior of the student. In addition to helping the student understand himself, the counselor needs to be involved in implementing change within the social setting. The change in attitude or behavior of the parents or teachers may be more effective in changing the student's self-concept and behavior than working with him in a counseling situation. Any realistic discussion of counseling must be concerned not only with counseling, but also with the practical aspects of manipulating, changing, or controlling the student's environment.

Consultation is based on the premise that the individual's self-concept and behavior are determined by his interactions with other people, and therefore a change in the way significant people respond to him will lead to a change in his behavior. Counseling may only be partially effective if behavior of teachers or parents is not changed. It is necessary to provide some assistance for the student. Because of his dependency, he is restricted from changing his environment alone. His behavior is limited by the restrictions put on him by adults. Therefore the counselor can work intensively with adults to change the student's environment.

Rotter (1954) suggests some general principles for consultation. First, the counselor helps teachers and parents to understand the effect of their behavior on the child's self-concept and behavior. Although it may be that they cause an undesirable behavior or a poor self-concept, blaming them would only stimulate guilt. Although it is difficult to help adults understand the interrelationship of their behaviors without placing blame on them, the counselor can reassure them by recognizing their good intentions and desire to help the student. It is more important to focus on changing the situation.

A second principle emphasizes leading, not pushing, the significant adult. An interpretation or suggestion is more likely to be accepted by the adult if he feels he has a major part in reaching the conclusion. The counselor can present information which helps the adults see the relationships between themselves and the student and ask them how they feel the child could be approached and then reinforce their appropriate suggestions.

Another principle involves dealing with facts that make sense to the adults. A counselor supports recommendations of the adults with information available to both of them. The adults can appraise the data and reach a conclusion in light of their own experience. The counselor can clarify the relationship between the reported behavior and the actual behavior of the student.

A fourth principle suggests that the counselor not go beyond the adult's potential ability for acceptance. When he leads the adults toward a certain conclusion, but meets resistance, it is better to retreat rather than to lose their cooperation. It is better to allow rejection of one idea than the whole process.

The counselor should establish an atmosphere in the consulting conference which permits the adult to feel free to express himself. If decisions are made, the adults should feel that they have had a part in making them. This process is aimed toward increasing their expectency that a change in their behavior will result in a better self-concept and more effective behavior for the student.

Consultation should take place in a period of joint diagnosis. The counselor is willing to come to the conference without a clear decision because of an underlying assumption that most parents or teachers will probably be more effective when they are able to identify the process between themselves and the student. The purpose of a joint diagnosis derives from the fact that the counselor will not know as much about the relationship between the people as the particular individuals involved. However, he can work as a consultant to help the parent or teacher become more aware of himself, the student, and their relationship. The counselor would not lead them to an action program, making suggestions about changing their relationship, until the other adult has done a thorough assessment of himself and the situation. The key assumption is that the other adult must perceive the problem himself to share the diagnosis and to be actively involved in generating a solution.

the school environment

The student cannot maintain his own self-image within the social environment, much less modify it, unless the social environment is compatible with his self-concept. This brings up a set of strategic questions and raises certain issues about social change. Can you insure lasting change in an individual without also changing the social situation? How are social systems changed so that individuals trust enough to give each other more autonomy and self-control and collaboration?

It has been stressed that one's self-concept is a learned perception and much of the teaching about one's self is done through interaction with significant others. Significant adults have influence on the formation and growth of self-concepts and behaviors of student. It should be of great concern to all educators that the school plays a major role in the development and reinforcing of self-concept, whether it is negative or positive. Additionally, it is necessary to recognize that negative self-concepts can be changed through meaningful school experiences. We must recognize that if self-image is born from social interaction, it can be reborn from social interaction. Jersild (1952), writing some twenty years ago, recognized that the school plays a vital role in the formation of self-concept, and challenged educators to use schools to promote self-understanding and -acceptance. The general thesis underlying his proposal was that human beings from an early age have more capacity for learning to face, understand, and deal constructively with the realities of life than adults assume.

If the school as a social environment can have an important influence on formation, reinforcement, and even change in self-concept, then the counselor cannot limit his repertoire to dealing with self-concept change in the counseling office. The counselor must look to the sociological aspects of his role.

Several authors have made a similar plea to counselors to widen their role to include the social change agent position. Weinberg (1968) stated that the counselor must be aware of social forces in the life of the student. Most counselors perceive solutions to student's problems through psychological means. If counselors would also begin to incorporate sociological dimensions of the role, they might supply schools with an agent of reconstruction and change. The guidance center could develop into a human resources center with counselors being involved in community problems as well as personal counseling. Warner and Hansen (1969) call for counselors, as the self-appointed change agents, to assume the responsibility for establishing a school evironment as a place where all students can have meaningful and significant experiences. That counselors have not played this role is attested to by professionals in other fields. Friedenberg (1959) asserts that adjustment is what guidance facilities try to assess and promote. The effect of this on the self-esteem of an adolescent who needs help badly can be disastrous. He already thinks ill of himself and is miserable about what he believes to be his deficiencies. According to Friedenberg, a student has reasons to be; the whole school, including the guidance department, contributes in large measure to and reconfirms many students' low self-esteem. Cicourel and Kitsuse (1963), after an extensive sociological research effort into determining the counselor role in the schools, suggested that the aim of counseling is to help students adjust to the school, and did not include at that time, and probably still does not in most schools, the function of examining the social structure of the school and the methods the school employs to educate the students.

In many cases the school actually stifles many of those it purports to serve. In practice, students are not only not encouraged to develop self-definition, but they are constantly pressured to think and act as the school mold dictates. The student who does not fit the mold, or who has either rejected the role and withdrawn from participation, or rejected the mold and become an outspoken critic of the system, is often thought of as having a problem.

What are some of the specific areas and techniques the counselor can employ within the context of extra counseling to improve or enhance the student's self-concept? The lockstep inflexibility of most school programs must be broken to give more attention to the needs of individual students. Herr (1969) suggested that educational programs must be created to match the needs and characteristics of students in continuous efforts to counteract the current, often pervasive, tendency to fit and force students into existing programs.

Curriculum has come to be seen as everything that takes place within the school, both formally and informally. Before counselors rush into involvement with curriculum reform in general, they must get their own house in order. What does the guidance program, as it now stands, do to enhance a student's self-concept? Are there objectives and priorities established within the guidance program that spell out the posture of the guidance functions? There are many current guidance practices existing in schools that help to form or reinforce negative self-concepts. How can these practices be supplemented with positive plans of action?

Most counselors can bear out Charles Silverman's findings as reported in *Crisis in the Classroom* (1970) that schools are "grim and joyless." Is it legitimate for a counselor to continue listening to student's concerns and continue seeing the obvious and expressed needs of students not being met without making some positive move in the direction of curriculum relevance? Almost twenty years ago, Ruth Strang (1954) warned that the counselor would find himself in a bad situation with clients if he helped them to discover their needs and then they found there were no provisions for meeting them.

The old model of adjusting the student to the curriculum, under which most counselors now labor, must give way to a new model of ajusting the school to meet the needs of the students. Many students cannot cope with the present curricular structure under which they find themselves, and their inability to cope with subject matter in schools certainly reduces their self-esteem.

An earlier chapter explored the effects of grading on self-concept, and the point was made that the developing self-concept of a student can be influenced by what the teacher says and does. The grade, as it is subjectively assigned by the teacher, becomes very important to the student's self-concept. Evaluation is a process of helping the student to examine and expand his own skills, and can involve the evaluation without reference to external standards or group comparisons. Without specific suggestions, we would suggest that the process of grading and evaluation be examined to determine if it is used to enhance the student's self-development or as a threat and contribution to negative self-development.

Ability grouping was also found to be a factor contributing to a negative self-concept. It is difficult for teachers to work with a variety of ability levels, yet they probably do so because many of the psychometric data used for grouping is neither accurate nor sufficient. Ability grouping is based primarily on conditions that call for education to be an information transmission activity. Students are preparing for life in the real world, so mastery of content is paramount. The concept of education for living now and that socialization and humanization are just as important as information must be implemented.

Discussion of grading systems and ability grouping leads to the concern with the old tradition of "healthy competition." Competition certainly exists in schools. It seems that most children come to school with the idea of competing for grades. Rosenberg (1965) notes that Margaret Mead suggested long ago that one of the characteristics of American middle-class child rearing practices is the pattern of "conditional love." Instead of accepting the child for what he is, Mead suggested that American parents show affection for the child when he outstrips others in some competitive enterprise and feel disappointed and distressed when he lags behind. It is not hard to infer what kind of unhealthy feelings and behaviors this kind of treatment can elicit from people. For some time, competition in schools was seen as a motivating force. But the same patterns of non-coping behavior exhibited in society and the business world are also evidenced in the schools. Cheating is very common, and the utter panic evidenced about getting into the right college points out that the artificial competition we have set up in our schools is not very healthy. This idea of competition as motivation should be reexamined. Competition in our schools turns out to be a motivation of limited value for some, and downright destructive for other (Combs, Avila and Purkey, 1971).

Cultural pluralism must become one of the aims or concerns of our schools. There is a close relationship between a learner's self-concept or self-identity and his academic achievement. Today cultural minorities are striving for self-identity. Our schools should expose the children to many different cultures rather than limiting them or just leaving them out (Ether, 1969).

Roth (1969) suggests that Negro children who are exposed to black studies improve their self-concept and black pride. This would affirm the belief that cultural pluralism should be advocated in the school program. Perhaps special studies is one avenue which can be taken to enhance the self-concept of the black children or any other minority group. Their frame of reference thus would be changed from the white to their own particular group. By enhancing self-concept, school achievement and personal growth would be facilitated and the individual then could realize his potential.

The ultimate objective of education is to enable each child to build a positive image of himself as a person. However, Morgan (1969) suggests that it would be destructive to these goals to implement remedial programs in education for the disadvantaged or to focus solely upon the development of narrowly defined cognitive skills. A disadvantaged child learns early who rules and controls the world, and realizes that the distance between himself and the rules will determine his destiny. As Morgan points out, minority groups must be liberated from feelings of inferiority and self-doubt. In order to accomplish this, he suggests information sharing at all levels which would bring schools in line with community, family, and individual needs.

conclusion

In changing self-perception toward more positive and effective living, it is important for someone to work with parents and teachers as well as with children. To assist parents, the school as well as other agencies in the community could assume this responsibility. Programs in parenthood, child development, personal development through groups, and understanding the world today are possibilities. For teachers, the administration, school psychologist, and counselors are in a position to offer varied kinds of assistance. Communication and understanding, both on an administrative and personal level, can be facilitated through group activities. For students, the combination of the administration, teachers, counselors, and school psychologists with the cooperation of parents can help the child toward positive perceptions of self. Essentially, what we are talking about is working toward good mental health in all people. Through interacting with each other in positive ways, self-concepts will be improved and behaviors will be more effective.

references

Carkhuff, R. *Helping and Human Relations, Vols. I and II.* New York: Holt, Rinehart & Winston, Inc., 1971.

———."Toward a Comprehensive Model of Facilitative Interpersonal Processes." *Journal of Counseling Psychology* 14 (1967): 67-73.

Carkhuff, R., and Berenson, B. *Beyond Counseling and Therapy.* New York: Holt, Rinehart & Winston, Inc., 1967.

Cartwright, D., and Zander, A. *Group Dynamics.* New York: Harper & Row, Publishers, 1968.

Cicourel, A. V., and Kitsuse, J. I. *The Educational Decision-Makers.* New York: The Bobbs-Merrill Co., Inc., 1963.

Combs, A. N.; Avila, D. L.; Purkey, W. W. *Helping Relationships: Basic Concepts for the Helping Professions.* Boston: Allyn & Bacon, Inc., 1971.

Cramer, S., and Herr, E. "Effecting a Rapproachement between Group Guidance and Group Counseling in the Schools." In *Group Guidance and Counseling in the Schools,* edited by J. Hansen and S. Cramer. New York: Appleton-Century-Crofts, 1971, 152-66.

Dollard, J., and Miller, N. *Personality and Psychotherapy.* New York: McGraw-Hill Book Company, 1950.

Ether, J. A. "Cultural Pluralism and Self-Identity." *Educational Leadership* 27 (December 1969): 232-34.

Friedenberg, E. Z. *The Vanishing Adolescent,* 2nd ed. Boston: Beacon Press, 1959.

Herr, E. "Guidance and Vocational Aspects of Education: Some Considerations," *Vocational Guidance Quarterly* 17 (1969): 178-84.

Holder, T.; Carkhuff, R.; Berenson, B. "Differential Effects of the Therapeutic Conditions upon High- and Low-Functioning Clients." *Journal of Counseling Psychology* 14 (1967): 63-66.

Jersild, A. T. *In Search of Self.* New York: Teachers College Press, 1952.

Kelman, H. C. "The Role of the Group in the Induction of Therapeutic Change." *International Journal of Group Psychology* 13 (1963): 399-432.

Loeser, L. "Some Aspects of Group Dynamics." *International Journal of Group Psychotherapy* 7 (1957): 5-19.

Morgan, H. "Demands for Recognition and Beyond." *Educational Leadership* 27 (December 1969): 229-31.

Piaget, G.; Berenson, B.; Carkhuff, R. "The Differential Effects of the Manipulation of the Therapeutic Conditions by High- and Low-Functioning Counselors upon High- and Low-Functioning Clients." *Journal of Consulting Psychology* 31 (1967): 481-86.

Rogers, C. "The Necessary and Sufficient Conditions of Therapeutic Personality Change." *Journal of Counseling Psychology* 21 (1957): 95-103.

Roth, R. W. "The Effects of 'Black Studies' on Negro Fifth Grade Students." *Journal of Negro Education* 38 (Fall 1969): 435-39.

Rotter, J. *Social Learning and Clinical Psychology.* Englewood Cliffs, N. J.: Prentice-Hall, Inc., 1954.

Rosenberg, M. *Society and the Adolescent Self-Image.* Princeton, N. J.: Princeton University Press, 1965.

Silberman, C. *Crisis in the Classroom.* New York: Random House, Inc., 1970.

Varenhorst, B., and Gelatt, H. "Group Guidance Decision-Making." In *Group Guidance and Counseling in the Schools,* edited by J. Hansen and S. Cramer. New York: Appleton-Century-Crofts, 1971, 107-123.

Warner, R. W., and Hansen, J. C. "Alienated Youth: The Counselor's Task." *Personnel and Guidance Journal* 48 (1970): 443-48.

Wolpe, J., and Lazarus, M. *Behavior Therapy Techniques.* New York: Pergamon Press, Inc., 1966.

Wrenn, G. "The Self-Concept in Counseling." *Journal of Counseling Psychology* 5 (1958): 104-109.

name index

Abernathy, Ethel, 49, 50
Adler, A., 5, 10, 11, 22
Angyal, A., 5, 22
Atkinson, C., 64, 75
Augustine, St., 2, 22
Auster, S.L., 68, 74
Ausubel, D.P., 28, 50
Avila, D.L., 98, 100
Back, K., 66, 74
Balthazar, E.E., 50
Baughman, E.E., 26, 41, 48, 50
Becker, E., 22
Bell, H., 76
Berenson, B., 80, 100
Blackman, L.S., 50
Borislaw, B., 61, 74
Brehm, M., 66, 74
Brookover, W.B., 6, 22, 37, 41, 58, 61, 74
Campbell, P.B., 60, 74
Carkhuff, R., 80, 83, 85, 100
Carlson, Rae, 48, 50
Carter, T.P., 65, 74
Cartwright, D., 86, 100
Chall, J., 75

Child, I.L., 28, 50
Cicourel, A.V., 96, 100
Clifford, C., 58, 59, 76
Cohen, J., 50
Combs, A.S., 5, 8, 22, 23, 54, 61, 74, 98, 100
Cooley, C.H., 6, 10, 15, 23
Coopersmith, S., 6, 23, 55, 61, 74
Cramer, S., 89, 100
Dahlstron, W.G., 50
Davidson, H.H., 33, 50, 64, 75
Dearden, M.H., 70, 75
Descartes, R., 2, 23
Diggory, J.C., 6, 23
Dollard, J., 80, 100
Donceel, J.F., 1, 23
Dorr, Mildred, 51
Edson, K., 76
Edwards, A.L., 51
Engel, Mary, 48, 51
Ether, J.A., 98, 100
Feder, D.D., 62, 76
Fhnk, M.B., 60, 75
Ford, D.H., 13, 23

Frank, Kitty F., 28, 51
Freud, Anna, 51
Freud, S., 7, 23
Friedenberg, E.Z., 96, 101
Fromm, E., 5, 23
Fromm-Reichmann, R., 55, 75
Gelatt, H., 88, 101
Goffman, E., 10, 18, 23
Goldstein, K., 5, 23
Green, R.L., 61, 75
Greenberg, J., 64, 75
Greene, B.I., 6, 7, 24, 31,
    51, 58, 75
Grever, J.M., 75
Hall, C.S., 11, 23
Halpern, F., 66, 75
Hamachek, D.E., 6, 23, 35, 47,
    51, 61, 75
Hansen, J.C., 96, 101
Havighurst, R.J., 42, 51
Herr, E., 89, 96, 100
Hilgard, E.R., 4, 23
Hill, W.T., 71, 75
Hogan, E.O., 61, 75
Holder, T., 82, 101
Horney, Karen, 5, 10, 12, 23,
    55, 56, 75
James, W., 3, 7, 23
Jersild, A.T., 27, 30, 33, 51,
    95, 101
Jordaan, J.P., 24
Jourard, S.M., 28, 36, 51
Kaplon, B.L., 56, 75
Kelman, H.C., 90, 101
Kinch, J.W., 23
Kitsuse, J.I., 96, 100
Kohlon, R., 67, 75
La Beene, W.D., 6, 7, 24, 31,
    51, 75, 88
Lang, G., 33, 50
Lazarus, M., 101
Lecky, P., 24, 42, 51, 58, 75
Levanway, R.W., 49, 51
Lewin, K., 5
Lewis, K., 24
Lindzey, G., 11

Locke, J., 2, 24
Loeser, L., 87, 101
Lynd, Helen M., 5, 24
Manis, J.G., 24
Maslow, A.H., 5, 24
McCandless, B.R., 27, 42, 51
McCelland, D.C., 5, 24
McCuen, J.T., 76
Mead, G.H., 10, 16, 24
Meltzer, B.N., 24
Miller, N., 80, 100
Monroe, R., 3, 24
Morgan, H., 99, 101
Osgood, C.E., 51
Osipow, S., 75
Patterson, A., 22
Piaget, G., 82, 101
Poussant, A.F., 64, 75
Purkey, W.W., 2, 24, 30, 37, 51,
    58, 75, 98, 100
Raimy, V.C., 24
Remy, R.M., 28, 51
Robinson, Myra Z., 51
Rogers, C.R., 5, 6, 9, 24,
    79, 101
Rosenberg, M., 34, 51, 55, 56,
    64, 75, 98, 101
Rosenberg, M., 34, 51
Rosenthal, Irene, 50
Roth, R.W., 98, 101
Rotter, J., 93, 101
Rozak, T., 40
Schpoont, S.H., 50
Schwieder, R.M., 67, 75
Secord, P.F., 36
Shaw, M.C., 60, 76
Sheldon, W.H., 51
Silberman, C., 97, 101
Snygg, D., 5, 6, 8, 24,
    54, 76
Staines, J.W., 33, 51
Stephenson, W., 52
Storm, T., 28, 50
Strang, Ruth, 97
Strong, O.J., 76
Suci, G.J., 51

Sullivan, H.S., 6, 10, 14, 24, 30, 52
Super, D.E., 24, 62, 76
Taba, Hilda, 42, 51
Tannenbaum, P.H., 51
Urban, H.B., 13, 23
Van Steinberghen, F., 25
Varenhorst, B., 88, 101
Viney, Linda 2, 25
Vostress, C.E., 64, 76
Warner, R.W., 96, 101

Washburn, W.C., 52
Wattenberg, W.W., 58, 59, 76
Welhowtz, Joan, 50
Welsh, G.S., 26, 41, 48, 50
White, R.W., 52
Wolpe, J., 80, 101
Wrenn, G., 62, 77, 101
Wylie, Ruth, 4, 5, 6, 25, 52, 59, 62, 76
Zander, A., 86, 100

subject index

Ability grouping, 31
Achievement, 58
Adolescent
  development, 34
  body image, 35
  parent influence, 37
  peers, 38
Affective discussion, 87, 89
Anxiety, 53-57
Behaviorism, 3-4
Body image, 35
Competition, 31-98
Consultation, 93
Counseling process
  action, 85
  facilitative condition, 81
  self-exploration, 82
  self-understanding, 84
Counseling relationship, 79
Defense processes, 43-47
Denial, 44
Disadvantaged, 63
Drug use, 66
Early philosophers, 2
Facilitative conditions, 81

Family Influence, 27, 37
Grading, 32
Group counseling, 86, 91
Group guidance, 88
Ideal self, 41
Individual counseling, 78
Life style, 11
Maintenance of
  self-concept, 42
Parental attitudes, 28
Peer relationships, 29, 31, 38, 39
Personifications, 14
Phenomenologists, 8
Projection, 46
Rationalization, 47
Reaction formation, 46
Repression, 44
School
  entering, 30
  ability grouping, 31
  teacher influence, 33
  grading, 32
School behavior, 57
School environment, 95
Self-understanding, 84

Self-exploration, 82
Self system, 15
Significant adults, 37
Social class, 65-66
Sociological theorists, 15-19

Social psychologists, 10
Stability of self-concept, 47
Symbolic interaction, 18
Teacher influence, 33
Vocational development, 62